AUTOGRAPH

A Complete Guide To 50 Proven Ways To
Improve Your Marriage

How To Fix Your Marriage
without using a hammer

FREE
Redeemable
"Love" Coupons
Inside

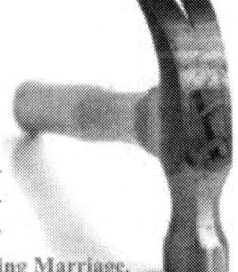

Whether You're Married or Contemplating Marriage,
This Is A 'Must Read' Book For Every Person.

Dr. Mikel Brown

CJ PUBLISHING COMPANY

EL PASO, TEXAS

How to Fix Your Marriage
Without Using a Hammer

1208 Sumac Drive
El Paso, TX 79925

Copyright © 2006 by Mikel Brown. All rights reserved
Printed in the United States of America
Library of Congress Control Number: 2006921119
ISBN: 9781930388130

Editorial assistance for CJC Publishing Co. by Gary Sparkman

Jacket design by C Hughes Advertising Agency

www.HowToFixYourMarriage.com
www.BuildingUWealth.com

All scripture references are from the King James Verison of the Bible unless otherwise noted.

No part of this publication may be reproduced, stored in a retrieval system, or transmitted in any form or by any means, electronic, mechanical, photocopying, recording, scanning, or otherwise, except as permitted under Section 107 or 108 of the 1976 United States Copyright Act, without either the prior written permission of the Publisher. Requests to the Publisher for permission should be addressed to the Permissions Department, CJC Publishing, 1208 Sumac Drive, El Paso, TX 79925, 915-595-1307, fax 915-595-1493, e-mail: permcoordinator@cjcpublishing.com.

Limit of Liability/Disclamier of Warranty: While the publisher and author have used their best efforts in preparing this book, they make no representation or warranties with respect to the accuracy or completeness of the contents of this book and specifically disclaim any implied guarantees. The advice and strategies contained herein may not be suitable for every situation. You should consult with a professional as it concerns your specific situation. Neither the publisher nor author shall be liable for any outcome concerning ones marriage or common law relationship, included but not limited to special, incidental, consequential, or other damages.

CONTENTS

Dedication..vi

Special Thanks..viii

Preface..ix

Chapter One
    What's In A Marriage..1

Chapter Two
    Before You Say, "I Do!"...13
    Premarital Evaluation
    Should We Try Living Together before Marriage?
    Determining If What You Feel is Real Love or Infatuation

Chapter Three
    Don't Marry A Child..39

Chapter Four
    Fixing You Is Draining Me...49
    The Secret Motive to Repair
    How Can I Change Me?

Chapter Five
    For Troubled Marriages..65

Chapter Six
       Successfully Overcoming The Pain of an Affair 79

Chapter Seven
       For Financially Challenged Marriages......................93

Chapter Eight
       Houston, We Have A Communication Problem.........105

Chapter Nine
       For Couples Who Can't Find The Time 115
       50 Things To Do To Produce A Quality Marriage

Chapter Ten
       For the Thrill Is Gone Marriage................................127

Chapter Eleven
       Pillow Talk...139
       For People Who Struggle with Sexual Gratification

Chapter Twelve
       Understanding How To Love Your Spouse................153

Chapter Thirteen
       Redeemable Love Coupons.....................................165

       "Quotes" For Marital Bliss...177

       About The Author..182

DEDICATION

This book is dedicated to my lovely wife, who has been my inspiration and dream come true. To my children whom I love with all my heart…you are my motivation. I cannot forget the many people that have allowed themselves to become my laboratory to develop and test ideas for helping to better their marriage. Keep growing!

SPECIAL THANKS

My heartfelt thanks and deepest appreciation to the following spiritual sons and daughters, and friends whose financial seeds have enabled the consummation of this project. I Love You!

Nicole Almeida
Charles & Talisha Bennett
Brian & Cindy Harris
Joshua & Shavon Boyd
The Harris Family
DeAndra & Melissa Hawkins
Victor Jackson
Savaslas & Tracey Lofton
Kevin & Andriea Cook

PREFACE

Marriage is definitely a labor of love and sometimes, more precisely, just plain hard work. However, the more work you put into your marriage the more joy you will receive out of it. So often couples point the finger of blame at their spouse as if he or she is solely responsible for the state of decay in the marriage. Not only is this unfair but it is also highly unlikely. Let's just keep it real, no one is all that! You both are a work in progress, flawed and imperfect. Can two flawed and imperfect people make a marriage work? Yes, absolutely, and without a doubt!

The release of this book is so timely. We live in a society that is so self-oriented. The "it's all about me" attitude is totally destructive to the very foundation of humanity which is marriage and family…What about US? The very concept of marriage implies it cannot possibly be an individual thing but it must be a partnership. Oh, now that is a refreshing thought! Many things are key to a successful partnership; communication, compromise, commitment, loyalty, reciprocity, clearly defined goals and plans, etc. Do not expect more from your spouse than you are willing to give. That is not a realistic or appropriate expectation. However, it is realistic for you and your spouse to agree on and honor the terms of the partnership. It requires that you be decisive and choose to do what is necessary to make your marriage a success. You must make your marriage your top priority.

Whether your marriage needs a tune up or a complete overhaul, this book will provide the information, as well as the inspiration, to achieve your happily ever after. Dr. Mikel Brown, who by the way is my pastor, my husband, and my very best friend, deals with the subject of fixing your marriage in such a practical, matter of fact, and easy to understand manner that despite the condition of your relationship, it can be repaired. Read with a heart of expectation, be willing to do your part, apply the principles provided, and you will discover your labor of love will become more love than labor.

Debra A. Brown

CHAPTER ONE

What's In A Marriage

*Falling in love is easy;
staying in love is laborious.*
*-- **Mikel Brown***

CHAPTER ONE

What's In A Marriage

All too often people enter the marriage covenant without understanding what the marriage institution is about and the principal foundation that governs it. I, too, was a victim of ignorance when it came to the marriage covenant. Like most people, I assumed that marriage was no more than bonding with your spouse, raising children, and growing old together. However, there are so many other important aspects that must be understood. Ambient factors exist that couples never figure on occurring or having to deal with. Falling in love is easy; staying in love is laborious. A marriage is more than just being in love. One must be conscious of how to love. Knowing how to love creates the security and the bond in order to maintain and grow a relationship.

The marriage institution is the single most important institution on earth, and it is frightening when you stop to think just how easy it is for people to secure a marriage license. To obtain a driver's permit, people must pass a rigorous driver's education course and or pass a driver's test to prove their road-worthiness, but there exist no qualifying measure to determine whether two individuals are marriage-worthy. Are legislators so blind as to think that marriages suffer no fatalities? The reason for this major lack of concern for this important institution, beyond keeping mere statistics, is that marriage is not fully understood by the lawmakers. The church has struggled in this area as well, due primarily to the mis-education of clergymen. Although marriage is not fully understood by many, it was once highly respected as an institution. In 1900, 709,000 marriages were tallied as opposed to only 55,751 divorces that same year. America reached its highest divorce rate in 1992. With 2,362,000 marriages starting in 1992, 1,215,000 of those ended tragically in divorce. A whopping sixty-five percent of all re-marriages in America deal with the issue of stepchildren and step parenting. Today, there are over 520,000 children in foster care. Thirty-five percent are White, forty-five percent are Black, thirteen percent are Hispanic, and six percent are Asian or other. The number of grandchildren living with their grandparents has risen from 3.2% in 1970 to 5.5% in 1997. These numbers speak volumes about the ignored epidemic in our society. Who's to blame for these staggering numbers of unfortunate circumstances? I'm sorry to say it, but broken homes equate to broken lives. The answer to America's and the world's dilemma is in educating the masses and developing the same standard across the board.

Nations, whose families are fragmented, have no continuity and their fabric is ripping at the seams.

Since America was founded on Christian values, would it not make sense to hold fast to principles that have guided this nation? As the American public wanders further away from its Christian roots, it is moving closer to its demise. We are destroying ourselves from within because we have depreciated the marriage institution–thus, weakening the backbone of this nation by dissolving our families. Nations, whose families are fragmented, have no continuity and their fabric is ripping at the seams. There is no other religious document in the world that reveals the origin of marriage and how to maintain its vitality, other than the Holy Bible. America's founding fathers held the Bible to be the guide for establishing this nation and writing the Declaration of Independence. After the American Constitution was written, George Washington and many other founding fathers felt that slavery was not compatible with the constitution and thus they felt that slavery should be abolished. George Washington, who owned slaves, vowed later in his life to never purchase another Black slave. These men were not perfect, nor did they live up to many of the Christian principles outlined in the Scriptures. They did, however, have a conscience that they felt needed to be guided by God, and not by some fictitious, conjured up deity. If we remove the Bible from the foundation of marriage, we will be left with nothing but empty, fragmented partnerships. Man did not and could not have thought of something so ingenious. God is the author and manufacturer of marriage. If you want to know how to fix your marriage, you must go to the manufacturer. God has all the solutions to all your marital problems.

In my reading of the Bible, it became apparent to me that the first marriage was not constituted under the primary guidelines of love. Somehow, we have failed to grasp the significance of why God brought the woman (Eve) to the man (Adam). The purpose for marriage is found in the reason God brought the woman to the man. Moreover, God did not say that Eve was Adam's wife; Adam declared it. God left the choice to Adam to join himself to Eve by his verbal declaration. The origin and history of the institution of marriage dates all the way back to man's original creation in Eden; this account is found in Genesis 2:18-25. From this passage we may develop the following principles:

(1) The unity of the man and woman is implied by her body being formed from his.
(2) Monogamy was God's original intention for marriage- one man joined to one woman.
(3) The social equality of husband and wife is presented.
(4) Subordination of the wife to the husband in terms of position not authority.
(5) The purpose for the union as mentioned by God.

The essence of the marriage ceremony consisted, in part, of the removal of the bride from her father's house to that of the bridegroom. You must recall in Genesis 1:26-28 how God created the spirit of both man and woman out of Himself. The house for the man (flesh) was created from the dust of the earth. Then God extracted the spirit of Adam from Himself and inserted it into the flesh by blowing into man's nostril, and then man became a living soul. Eve's spirit was still inside of God because the Bible is clear on the fact that the first physical specimen was Adam. God made the house of the woman from Adam's rib, and as with Adam, God inserted Eve's spirit into the body of the woman. The point is simple. Eve left the Father's bosom and was joined to her husband, and the two of them became one flesh. Please note from the Scriptures that Adam stated that they were one flesh, not one spirit. Eve did not come from Adam's spirit; she was of his flesh. Her spirit came from God who is the Father of spirits. (Hebrews 12:9)

The primary ingredient in marriage is purpose. What is

the purpose for coming together in matrimony with another human being? We cannot say that love was the driving force behind God making Eve for Adam because Adam was totally unaware of Eve's existence until God brought her to him. So then, what should be the reason for a man and woman coming together in marriage today? The answer is discovered in Genesis 2:20, when God announced the purpose of producing the woman. Every creation of God has meaning for its design. God creates nothing without first having a purpose given for its existence. Eve's purpose was not mainly for companionship and procreation. For we know that consenting adults can produce children without being married. Animals are constantly producing other animals, but you will never read anywhere in the Bible where God joins two animals in marriage. God did not create the marriage institution for the sake of procreation alone.

> ***A marriage is not held together simply because it is an institution; it is held together because of its right content.***

Marriage is an umbrella that a man and a woman come under in order to fulfill God's plan in the earth. The woman is an architectural ornament produced so that God's glory (man) can have help (woman) to represent and rule a kingdom on earth as God rules in heaven. Sex is not the reason for man and woman committing to each other in marriage; it is the method used to solidify or to consummate the marriage. Adam's verbal acceptance of Eve authorized them to have intercourse in order to perfect the marriage process, not as the reason for simply making babies. When sex is the driving force for marriage, then sex becomes the foundation for the marriage. And as the sexual appetite begins to dissipate over the years, the marriage vow is weakened. Therefore, the marriage has no integrity or super glue to hold the marriage bond together. Since sex, and not God's purpose, is the adhesive used to hold many of today's marriages together, many cannot hold up under the weight of society's many pressures. Marriage was not designed to work under selfish motives.

When a man and a woman decide to become joined in holy matrimony, the decision to do so should be made with the full understanding of the divine purpose for being married. When this is comprehended, individuals will not compete with each other, misunderstand their roles, or conform to secular standards. Therefore, any temporary disunity, disunion or disruption will not be strong enough to eat away at their verbal and spiritual bond. A marriage is not held together simply because it is an institution; it is held together because of its right content. Just as an automobile is designed to run on gasoline, a marriage is designed to work under its true purpose. If a person fills his gas tank with a favorite flavored soda pop, it would be ludicrous to wonder what is wrong with his car when the engine ceases to operate. This individual should not expect his engine to run smoothly, despite using his favorite soda pop. People are using the wrong ingredients for their marriages and are wondering

Marriage is not a war; it is a love affair.

why the marriages aren't working. It is not the marriage that is not working; it is what individuals are pouring into their marriages.

How To Fix Your Marriage

The next ingredient is the most complicated subject of the marriage dilemma. Since each party to a relationship usually tends to establish a certain mental framework based on the initial cues received from the other, it is difficult to discuss this particular subject without causing some eyebrows to rise. When the primary issues in marriage cause individuals to fixate on what is not being received, then it is apparent that giving is not the central theme. This subject touches on love because selfless giving is the quintessential of what love is all about in a relationship. Are you ready? Can you honestly receive this vital information without pointing the finger at your spouse? Again, I ask, are you ready? U-N-S-E-L-F-I-S-H-N-E-S-S! There, I said it. Unselfishness is a vital ingredient in order for the marriage covenant to work. Usually, when I mention this word in discussions with couples, individuals are quick to say, "You hit the nail on the head!" One is quick to point the finger without realizing that there are four fingers pointing back at the critical spouse.

People are usually not willing to admit their shortcomings in front of their spouses for fear that the disclosed information might be used as ammunition against them in their next confrontation. Marriage is not a war; it is a love affair. Marriage is not established on the give me first attitude. God constructed Eve for the sake of giving to Adam what was missing, and Adam was to give to Eve what was needed. "It is not good that man be alone" was what God said. Therefore, God physically designed Eve so that Eve could meet a need in Adam's life. But what was the need in Eve's life that Adam was designed to satisfy? The answer is in the Scriptures. Adam was physically manifested first in order to give love and guidance to those who would follow. Adam was to provide Eve with love, security, and leadership. I am not saying that Adam was Eve's supervisor. What I am saying is that Adam represents the personage of God on planet Earth. He is the person designed by God to meet the needs of the woman. Adam's job is not to control or dominate the woman in any way. He is merely to provide leadership, and leadership ceases to have meaning when there is no one willing to follow.

Adam loved Eve, and Eve was to respect and honor the position of her husband. A true marriage exists when two people have mutual love and respect for who their spouse is presently, not ideas of what he or she may want the other to become.

Jotting Down Things to Remember

Jotting Down Things to Remember

Jotting Down Things to Remember

CHAPTER TWO

Before You Say, "I Do!"

Expecting success without preparation is like preparing without an agenda.
 -- Mikel Brown

CHAPTER TWO

Before You Say, "I Do!"

Before saying, "I do" to their future life partners, there are many things that individuals need to consider. One must understand that once the wedding vows have been exchanged and intercourse has sealed those vows, two individuals, with once separate lives, are now joined together for life. This sobering truth should cause all couples to carefully examine every aspect of the institution of marriage before deciding to tie the knot.

As a counselor with over twenty-five years of premarital and marriage counseling under my belt, I have personally experienced just about every situation imaginable. From spousal murder to marital bliss and everything in between, I have seen it all. To keep it real, I guess you could say that I've done that, been there and have the T-shirt to prove it. As far as marriage goes, I know what will work, what won't work, and what should never be attempted. So, if you would like to increase the odds of enjoying greater success in your marriage, apply the premarital principles outlined in this particular chapter; you'll be glad you did. The primary reason most couples live with the specter of doom hanging over their marriages is that they fail to employ crucial prerequisites that lead to blissful unions. Expecting success without preparation is like preparing without an agenda.

Allow me to tell it like it is. At least ninety-five percent of couples contemplating marriage are completely blinded by what I call "temporary insanity." By temporary insanity I am referring to the willful disregard for those obvious signposts that jump out to alert us to potential problem areas in a relationship. No one knows for sure what his/her partner is thinking, unless he/she has the ability to read minds. Yet, this propensity to assume what the other is thinking causes "reality" to become the first casualty in relationships- doubly so in marriage. Consequently, large percentages of potentially great marriages end in divorce because of unsubstantiated assumptions.

Rather than probe for the truth prior to getting married, most engaged couples opt instead to remain in the dark about serious issues that should be addressed prior to jumping the broom (getting married). This occurs primarily because people are naïve enough to believe that love alone will rectify or smooth over every problem brought from dating into marriage. Hogwash! Men and women in dating relationships are the best actors I have ever seen. Their performances are deserving of an Oscar because pretending (and not offending) is what many people do while courting. While no one wants to offend his/her prospective spouse, being truthful, open and honest sometimes does just that. And because individuals in dating situations are most susceptible to buying into false pretenses, they must learn to be more discerning in order to safeguard against future devastation. Why? Because your heart will recover from the hurt of being deceived, but your future condition will be forever shaped by today's decisions.

How To Fix Your Marriage

No one consciously or intentionally sets out to make bad decisions regarding life. We would all like to believe that we have carefully weighed the pros and cons before embarking on such a profoundly life-altering journey as marriage. In fact, the complete opposite is true. Most people seek very little counsel and advice concerning the decision to marry or the person they intend to marry. Love-inspired warnings from parents to their sons and daughters about their future spouses are usually met with feelings on the part of the children that the parents are just trying to invade and control their lives or that the parents are too old-fashion and out of step with modern times.

The truth is that young adults today find very little reason to follow any advice when they have observed for years the failed state of their parents' marriages. They see little need to duplicate the plethora of failed images of marriage that exist in our society. In order for parents to be able to weigh in with the vital input that is needed, they must first paint the picture of marriage success that our children can trust and be inspired to want to emulate.

Attention!!! Attention!!! Attention!!! I'm sounding this clarion alarm to anyone seriously interested in protecting a future investment of time, resources, and energy. This call goes out to young ladies and young men, divorcees and the widowed. Hearken to my admonition while you yet have time to save the rest of your life. Don't get me wrong, marriage is beautiful when two people are willing to surrender completely their individual wills to one another. Conversely, it can be hell on earth if either both or one person in the marriage is unwilling to yield to the needs of the other.

I once heard Mrs. Huxtable (character on the successful '80s and '90s sitcom *The Cosby Show*) say to one of her children that "Marriage is both partners giving 50 percent." Although hilariously entertaining, the Huxtable family did not accurately portray the inner dynamics of most families nor did it offer any practical solutions for how individuals could obtain long term marital success. Fifty plus fifty may equal one hundred, but to suggest that individuals surrender these fractional amounts as adequate contributions to a relationship is to further suggest that each person need only put out half the effort to achieve success in marriage. This doesn't sound like the proper prescription for a winning relationship to me.

Each partner must contribute one hundred percent effort in order for marriage to work. Just because you may say "I do," doesn't mean you will when the proverbial rubber meets the road. "I do" must mean "I will" under all circumstances in order for "I do" to take on meaningful significance as a wedding vow. It takes all that two people have in terms of love, energy, resources and surrendered will in order for any partnership to truly work. So, before you say "I do", determine how much of "I do" you are actually willing to commit to do.

Okay, I know you are probably saying enough! "Get to the meat so that I can make a well-informed and calculated decision. Hurry, because I have only an hour to make my decision." Why would you relegate something so important to only a few minutes of careful evaluation? There is no hard and fast rule that defines how much pre-marital inspection time is sufficient for learning about your potential spouse before agreeing to say "I do." But there are questions that should be answered before you make a lifetime commitment to another. Well, let's find out where you stand in the estimation of making a wise and intelligent decision.

Premarital Evaluation

"Efforts and courage are not enough without purpose and direction." --John F. Kennedy

In order to properly assess where you are, you must answer the following questions as truthfully as possible. I emphasize candor here because people are usually quick to respond to questions of this nature without carefully considering their answers. This occurs for two main reasons. First, respondents may feel threatened by the probative nature of the questions asked of them. Secondly, these questions cause individuals to come face-to-face with the painful reality that they may not be as mature, at that moment, to take on the responsibilities of marriage- not an easy notion to ponder.

Question 1:

Why do you want to be married?

Carefully consider your reason(s) for wanting to be married. Don't think about your potential spouse right now; think only of yourself at this time. People get married for any number of reasons.

- Loneliness (Loss of direction)
- Sex (Lack of fulfillment)
- Companionship (Loss of identity)
- Money (Lack of fulfilled potential)
- Trophy (Need for challenge)
- Children (Loss of parental focus)
- Debt (Lack of discipline)
- Love (Misunderstood potential)
- Other (You name it)

For instance, if you think that love is the only reason for marriage, you are sadly mistaken. If you can't define love in practical terms, stating it as one of your reasons for wanting to get married, it might be a bit naïve. What many people consider love is not true love at all. In many instances people misconstrue sexual attraction as love. Consequently, these individuals make decisions to commit to another based on this feeling alone. When sex becomes the basis for two people coming together, it usually will not endure the pressures of life because the glue that is supposed to exist between husband and wife is not strong enough to keep them together during life's trials.

Loneliness **is not a lack of companionship; it is a loss of direction.** If you think that another person being in the same house with you is the answer to your lonesomeness, you may be surprised to discover that there are multitudes of lonely individuals living in the same house with their spouses. As incredible as it may seem, it is still possible to experience loneliness in marriage, especially if the partners never cultivate healthy communication.

Sex **should never be the major reason for two people coming together in marriage, but it should be a main staple in a healthy one.** Sexual intercourse is a vital component of any marriage, and it serves several important functions from procreation to fostering intimacy to relieving built up stress.

When two people love each other, it is only natural for them to want to give themselves to each other sexually because, after all, it is the highest level of intimacy two people can experience. Problems surface, however, when sex becomes the only thing keeping two people together. When this is the case, a relationship is destined for a rollercoaster ride. What becomes the status of a once satisfying sexual relationship when the pedestrian affairs of marriage (raising children, working, and paying bills) begin to compete for a couple's intimate moments or when one partner can no longer fulfill that particular obligation, owing to injury or a debilitating disease? When the sex ends, does love end also? If sex is the only glue holding two people together, marriage is destined to fall apart when the glue is gone.

Companionship is valuable, but not critical.

Most couples do confess in counseling sessions that their sexual relationships become routine and lack luster after only one year of marriage. For women, the desire for sex reduces considerably after the first child is born, and they adjust mentally to marriage much differently than do men. While women tend to enjoy the fact of being married, men tend to find enjoyment in reminiscing about the good old days of dating. In instances where couples have engaged in premarital sex, the husband is usually the one who tries to resurrect the thrill of those sexual feelings derived during courtship.

***Companionship* is valuable, but not critical.** If the need for companionship is the overriding reason for an individual choosing to marry, such desire may signal the birth of a needy, high-maintenance partner in the making. Such individuals are usually loquacious and very nagging. Please do not misconstrue my statement as being insensitive and disconcerting. This type of personality is generally someone who was deprived of amity or at least they thought they were.

***Money* is a bad reason to pursue marriage, but don't downplay its importance**. If you marry someone who is financially strapped, odds are your life will probably be in constant want of life's basic necessities.

Tension in a family is bound to reach the boiling point when a husband, wife and children are constantly struggling to secure and subsist on the bare essentials. Money does not discriminate in its ability to be a blessing or curse to its owner. While we commonly look to the lack of money as being the source of most of our woes, tremendous financial prosperity carries with it, its own set of problems and temptations. Although most married couples typically start out at the lowest rungs of the financial ladder, they usually progress up the ladder as a result of improved economic conditions. It is important that they pursue understanding and wisdom so they would know how best to manage the increased wealth entrusted to their stewardship.

***Trophies* are items such as metals or prizes that people acquire for winning or accomplishing a particular feat.** Some individuals enjoy the challenge of winning another's love. To them, this is a prize worth pursuing.

While pursuing the love of another person is never wrong, we must be careful not to focus more on the trophy (landing a spouse) without considering the entire bounty that goes along with gaining a wife or husband— bounty such as the need to nurture the relationship, sacrificing for your mate, and providing for their needs. When a person becomes the object of a focused pursuit, there exists a strong tendency to neglect the trophy once the prize is won. In this case, marital infidelity can result as the hunter needs new prey upon which to set his/her sights, if certain passions are not placed under control.

***Children* should never be a primary reason for marriage**. Producing children should never be the sole reason for wanting a spouse. If it is, the spouse you eventually get will always be an incidental part of your life- second always to your child.

Wanting a spouse simply for the sake of having children is like putting the cart before the horse. In cases where the baby's father is not in the picture, women are prone to gauge each potential spouse by his ability to be a good step-father and not necessarily by his ability to be a good husband. Eyeing a potential husband in this fashion does great injustice to any potential marriage relationship. While being a good father is crucial, women must first demand that a potential mate exhibit qualities that point toward his being a good husband. Remember that long after the children are gone, husband and wife will still be in each other's lives.

***Debt*, which may indicate the symptom of uncontrolled spending habits, is one of the three major factors that contribute to the high rate of divorce in our society.** Debt is like a drug. Some people want to be freed from it but feel as though they can't live without it. People under the weight of serious debt usually find themselves struggling with integrity issues. Debt is not just a symptom; it is also a debilitating condition of the mind.

***Love* seems like the logical and biblical reason for marriage**. During times of antiquity, marriages were not based on love but on arrangement. Couples clearly understood then that love was a process that took time to truly blossom, and they knew too that marriage was an arrangement that made good economic and practical sense. I am not saying that love should not be considered. What I am saying is that it should not be the only consideration.

Loving a person doesn't mean that the one you love is the best individual with whom to spend the rest of your life. You may love a person based on how he or she makes you feel, but there are serious matters that one must consider. What if the person has some serious issues, such as a drug or alcohol addiction? The individual may even be a sluggard who is not motivated to pursue any productive enterprises. Perhaps, the person may have an issue with anger management. You might marry him or her because you love the individual, but eventually you will regret the day you ever said "I do."

The truth is that we marry people for various reasons, and each one of the reasons previously addressed must be examined on the strength of its own merit and not taken out of context. Balance and maturity will dictate the priority that individuals place on the reasons they have for wanting to enter the estate of holy matrimony. When individuals approach the institution of marriage with this sober understanding, then and only then can they truly be to their spouse what they were intended to be.

Question 2:

How much personal information am I willing to offer so that my potential spouse can make a fair and balanced assessment of my entire life- past, present and future?

It is unfair for you not to disclose detailed and very private information about your life to the person you intend to marry. You must summon courage to share even those past traumatic experiences that have caused you tremendous pain because our pasts have a way of reaching into our present to try and rob us of peace, joy and happiness. Avoiding the discussion of personal problems before marriage will not eliminate the strong possibility of them showing up after you're married. Let your potential spouse know about your private pains and things you've suffered in the past so that he or she won't be blind-sided by issues that may later surface in the marriage. The Latin phrase caveat emptor ("let the buyer beware") should apply to marriage as well as to financial transactions.

Question 3:

Does your potential spouse avoid answering painful questions?

> **The secret pains of your potential spouse will eventually become your public war, if you don't take steps to address them.**

I once counseled a divorced couple who contemplated remarriage. The woman expressed her concerns about his fidelity during their separation, but he was very reluctant to account for his actions during this time. So, I probed and asked him why he refused to address her concerns. He replied, "I have been forgiven, and it therefore should not be mentioned again." My reply was simple but harsh. "A man can be forgiven for adultery, but if he contracted AIDS in the process, it shouldn't be dismissed, but rather discussed."

Needless to say, she remarried him anyway. A year later, she filed for divorce a second time after he caused her tremendous financial distress because of a serious drug abuse problem. The secret pains of your potential spouse will eventually become your public war, if you don't take steps to address them.

Question 4:

Is your future spouse willing to be open about their sexual affairs?

Investigate, but don't interrogate!

I believe the answer given in question three can help you deal with this question. But allow me to add just a little more information concerning this question. I do not believe that every detail of a person's sexual escapades before marriage should be discussed. On the other hand, I do believe that one should disclose the approximate number of sexual partners one may have slept with during their singleness. The reason being is that, in addition to the possibility that some sexually transmitted disease could have been contracted during this time, there may exist some underlying reasons that caused one partner to feel the need to experience multiple sex partners prior to marriage. While not a reason to pull out of the wedding, an over-active sex life prior to marriage and the reasons for it must be carefully weighed and considered.

Don't be afraid to ask the question, what do you believe led you to having multiple sexual partners? If the person answers truthfully and you feel certain that the individual has resolved his/her issues in the area of sex, it may be worth laying the issue to rest and progressing further toward marriage. If, on the other hand, you don't feel comfortable with the answers offered, you may want to halt any further steps toward the altar because marital infidelity may be the result. Investigate, but don't interrogate! Ask questions with a loving considerate concern, not with a malicious deception to prove your suspicion. If the potential spouse feels that he or she is being cross-examined, that person may not answer truthfully and will perhaps resent you in the process.

Question 5:

Do you know about the childhood experiences of your future spouse?

Good, bad, or indifferent, people are shaped by their experiences. It must be understood that humans have the propensity for repeating previous events. It is important that we know the childhood experiences that have impacted the lives of the people we care about because they are what serve to shape the character of every individual. For example, if your potential spouse grew up resenting his or her parents; he or she may subconsciously transfer that same resentment into your marriage and direct those negative feelings toward you and your children.

It matters greatly if a person was molested, raped, or physically abused as a child. I believe to some extent that most people come from dysfunctional families. We've all grown up with siblings and other relatives who were either drunkards, prostitutes, drug abusers, thieves, habitual liars or con artists. Most instances of molestation directed against children are perpetrated by a trusted family member. When this kind of trust is betrayed, individuals tend to become withdrawn, less trusting, and generally suspicious of all people, even sincere loved ones.

Question 6:

Have you investigated your potential spouse's financial intelligence?

Most couples start their relationships with a great deal of kissing and hugging, and choose to remain in the clouds regarding very practical financial matters that will affect their relationships for a long time. When money is finally

> *Financial illiteracy helps to form an unhealthy attitude about money.*

considered, it is usually too late. If one of the future spouses is financially astute, there is hope. But if both are young and financially illiterate, then they are in for a difficult and long journey.

If the person you are contemplating marrying lacks the aggression needed to provide a comfortable home for you and the children, then they may be prone to create a financial deficit so deep that you will not be able to climb out on your own. Financial illiteracy helps to form an unhealthy attitude about money. Never allow love to blind you to the realization of your need for money. Love will quickly fizzle out when there is no income to fill a home with furniture, a kitchen with food, and a garage with a reliable vehicle. Money is one of the top three leading causes of divorce.

Question 7:

Do you have any marriage reservations due to trust issues with your future spouse?

If you have the slightest uncertainty in your mind or heart, don't make a move until you are mentally clear and spiritually coherent to make the proper decision. It is better to defer the pain of a bad decision than to regret having made such a painful choice.

Question 8:

Have you been sexually active with your potential spouse?

Please do not have any reservations about answering this question truthfully because chances are I will never know. The only ones who need ever know something as intimate as this are you, your potential spouse and God. I am

> *Trust is the foundation for a long, healthy relationship.*

not a relationship police in my off-duty time, just waiting to arrest individuals who commit infractions of biblical proportions. I've asked this question for a reason- not to make you feel guilty for not waiting until marriage or for your lack of understanding as to why you should.

Premarital sex sets the stage for the occurrence of unfaithfulness later in the relationship. In over eighty percent of marriages rocked by adultery, one or both spouses

> *Premarital abstinence may not be the popular thing to do, but it will certainly prove to be the right thing.*

admitted to having premarital sex. Trust is the foundation for a long, healthy relationship. Suspicion arises out of distrust. Suspicions are amplified when, for whatever the reason, insecurity sets in and the insecure spouse has, as a mental backdrop, memories of his or her premarital sexcapades. The person may begin to reason that if my spouse had premarital sex with me, what will keep him/her from engaging in sex with someone else now that we are married. Sadly, the likelihood of marital infidelity increases drastically in cases where couples have been sexually active prior to marriage.

Question 9:

Have you been pressured by your potential spouse to engage in sexual intercourse?

If having sex matters more to your potential spouse than your desire to save yourself for the wedding night, then that individual neither loves you nor is he or she concerned about your convictions. Testing the sexual waters prior to marriage, so to speak, is no indicator for how fulfilling a marriage relationship will or will not be; although, some people are naïve enough to believe the contrary. Truth has shown that when a person compromises a deeply felt standard, the other partner soon discovers that the line in the sand can shift easily with a little pressure. And before long, all kinds of unreasonable expectations are brought before the one who once lived a principled life.

Should We Try Living Together Before Marriage?

I am not surprised by the increasing number of individuals who choose to live together before marriage. The reason often cited is that they want to be absolutely certain that this is the right person before they say "I do" for a lifetime. While these individuals may feel that they are only testing the water, they are in fact hurting, not helping, their marriage prospects.

Under these kinds of premarital living arrangements, marriages are significantly more likely to end in divorce. This is partly because people who choose to live together

> *It is not until you are fully immersed in the commitment of marriage that you can appreciate its benefits.*

tend to be younger, less committed to biblical principles or have other qualities that put them at higher risk for divorce. Marriage is a solemn covenant between committed individuals and that is not possible to sample by pre-marriage, live-in arrangements. Though I agree that marriage must be entered into wisely, testing the waters by living with a potential spouse will never produce the right conditions to simulate what marriage is truly like. It is not until you are fully immersed in the commitment of marriage that you can appreciate its benefits.

Many people enter cohabitate relationships where the understanding is that if the arrangement doesn't work, we can split up and go our separate ways because we do not have a legal commitment. This type of commitment is no real commitment at all. But it is this type of thinking that contaminates and ruins many marriages.

A report was done based on a survey of nearly 11,000 women. The study found that by age 30, three in four women have been married and half have lived with a partner outside marriage. It identified numerous risk factors that make certain groups more prone to divorce: (1) People who are young, (2) low incomes, (3) no religious affiliation, (4) little education, and (5) children of divorced parents. Overall, 43 percent of marriages break up within 15 years, according to data from the National Survey of Family Growth. Black women are least likely to marry and most likely to divorce, with more than half splitting within 15 years. Asian marriages are the most stable, with Whites and Hispanics in between. Women are waiting longer to get married than they used to, and after a divorce, they are less likely to remarry than women once were.

The survey, released by the Centers for Disease Control and Prevention, found that 70 percent of those who lived together for at least five years did eventually walk down the aisle. But these marriages lack longevity and are more likely to break up. After 10 years, 40 percent of couples that had lived together before marriage ended in divorce. That compares with 31 percent of those who did not live together prior to marriage. A big reason for such disparity in these statistics may be found in the difference in outlook of those who choose to cohabit versus those who believe that the commitment of marriage is the way to go. When individuals live together in cohabitation arrangements, they tend to approach lifelong commitment to one person half-heartedly based on whether their partner makes them happy or not.

Marriage is not about having different expectations of what the commitment is all about. If one of the partners believes that marriage requires full commitment and surrender while the other views it as simply a way to save money by just splitting the cost of rent, then the two people are in for a rude awakening after "I do" has been vowed. A report, based on 1995 data, identified young adults as a group that poses a particularly high risk of experiencing divorce. Nearly half of those who marry under age 18 and 40 percent under age 20 get divorced. For those over age 25, the figure falls to just 24 percent. The difference in maturity levels are,

I'm certain, the primary factor leading to the reduced incidences of divorce among older individuals.

Older people tend to approach life with a more balanced perspective when it comes to dealing with the issues of life– this as a result of having simply experienced more in life than younger individuals. As a result, older couples tend to focus more on those relationship issues that matter most, rather than fixating on the most trivial differences. Older couples also tend to have more at stake as their investment of time and resources is greater than that of younger individuals. This explains why older people are more tenacious when it comes to fighting to preserve their precious unions.

There are moral imperatives that account for why some groups fare better at marriage than others. The Bible defines the parameters of marriage, and it also spells out certain roles that a husband and wife are to fulfill. Research reveals that people who look to the Bible as the basis for fulfilling the marital responsibilities, view marriage as a holy covenant not to be entered into lightly and dissolved only under the narrowest of guidelines. As a result, couples tend to remain married longer when religion plays a major part of their overall lives. An interesting statistic shows that among people who don't consider themselves part of any religious group, 46 percent get divorced within 10 years. Women whose parents were divorced are significantly more likely to divorce themselves, with 43 percent splitting after 10 years. Among those whose parents remained together, the divorce rate was just 29 percent.

I am not suggesting that religion is the answer to bringing down the divorce rate. The explanations are not that simple. People are complex creatures with a great deal of uncertainty and unpredictability about them. Life tends to cause individuals with good hearts and great intentions to become weighed down by many cares and troubles that cause people to lose their way. On the other hand, being completely rooted in and committed to Jesus Christ does guarantee His followers that they will stay on the straight and narrow path that leads to life eternal. Can they decide how their spouse is going to live and conduct their lives? No! Each person is completely responsible for his or her own actions. Broken relationships do not always lead to divorce. Many couples separate, but remain legally married. Some couples cohabitate in the same house but choose to live in different rooms. These individuals tend to never divorce because they believe in the sanctity of marriage. However, their ignorance of marriage from God's standpoint keeps them from fully enjoying their marriages as they should.

> *An infatuation is an illusion of a self-manufactured assumption.*

Determining If What You Feel is Real Love or Infatuation

It is frightening to think that romance can cause two people to lose their sensibilities and disrupt sound decision making. But feelings of love and infatuation have this very effect on people when they get swept away in a torrent of emotions. How is it possible for two people to get so caught up in some strange unseen power? The attraction to another is very real, but most people do not allow infatuation to give way to the substantive reality of love. And it is infatuation that causes most people to make serious commitments before love has a chance to settle in.

An infatuation is an illusion of a self-manufactured assumption. When it surfaces, it is usually the most ideal and fondest thoughts of another person. Infatuation appears as the initial stage of fascination, and it is this fascination that draws two people toward one another. The term infatuation means to be carried away by fanatical passions. It is initially engaging each other in a psychological affair. Infatuation is just that, an affair of the mind. It offers no more than a fantasized relationship which often ends up going no where. Pursuing the object of infatuation is like trying to build a house of shifting sand.

Marriage is love, and love is blinding. Therefore, marriage is an institution for the blind. Laugh, it's a joke. In reality, a person would be quite silly to base a relationship on feelings and appearance. True love should always be tested and proven based on how you see your future mate not by how you want to see them. You should never close your eyes to their human flaws with the thought that you can change them. Real love accepts a person along with his or her imperfections. You must safeguard against trying to force your spouse to change into someone they were never meant to become. If you're not careful, your entire marriage may become polluted with constant complaints of disapproval.

How can I know if it's real love or just some childish romantic fascination? Life holds no guarantees or promises. People are not immutable in their character. In life, some people experience true love and others never do. Those who do not often enter into relationships thinking that love will eventually be the outcome if only they could do something to earn or deserve it. For them, love is viewed as a reward gained in exchange for something else. Pure, unconditional love is something they cannot conceive. Subsequently, the love which the person has never received is precisely the love they are unable to give.

Several years ago, a young Hispanic woman thought that she had fallen in love with a young man who appeared to be very nice and gentle. Over time, he eventually won her confidence. She was, however, naïve and totally oblivious to his sinister nature. He seemed to be so honest and open about his life that she felt that he could never be the kind that he turned out to be. After he pushed with subtle pressure for them to engage in intercourse, she gave in and committed her body to him. Although she wasn't comfortable, she was confident that he was the right man for her. After several sexual episodes, she became pregnant. When she made him aware of the pregnancy, he grew angry and argued that the baby was not his. He left her and used "the baby is not my baby" excuse in order to ease his conscience of any wrong doing. He left her wounded, hurt, and despondent. Her self esteem was savagely wounded and got to the point where she didn't want to live.

After several months had passed, she allowed another young man to come into her life. He didn't seem to care about her being pregnant. He claimed to love her regardless of her misfortunes and abandonment. He demonstrated patience with her during her second trimester. And once again she became confident of his feigned genuine concern. But she was unaware of the deep rooted problems of violence that surrounded this young man's life. This time her relationship would become a near fatal experience.

He began to feel as though he had demonstrated enough love for her and that she needed to return the favor by engaging in sex, despite being pregnant. She informed him of her desire to be with him, but she had no desire to engage in intercourse until the baby was born. This young man thought that sex was the ultimate expression of love and he demanded it now more insistently. He was relentless and down right frightening at times, but his anger would subside, as he regained his calm.

One day, fed-up with the constant rejection of his advances, he went into the kitchen, pulled a knife out of the drawer and commenced to cutting and stabbing her. He cut and stabbed her thirty-seven times. She survived this ordeal, but her life and trust in men is to this day completely destroyed. Psychiatric assistance was needed in order to nurse this woman back to a state of mental well-being. Her near fatal wounds were not nearly as deep as the mental wounds she had encountered.

Nowadays, protecting yourself against unsavory characters is vitally important before becoming too entwined in a relationship. Domestic violence has crossed all racial, socio-economic, and gender lines. No group is exempt from this monster that seems to slip into relationships unaware. Don't be afraid to do some extensive investigation of the individual you plan to marry because if you are going to spend the rest of your life with another person, you may as well experience the peace and joy that marriage is supposed to offer.

Jotting Down Things to Remember

Jotting Down Things to Remember

CHAPTER THREE

Don't Marry A Child

Children lack the maturity to fully weigh the consequences of their actions. Therefore, if you desire a spouse, find a responsible man or woman, not a boy or girl.
*-- **Mikel Brown***

CHAPTER THREE

Don't Marry A Child

I would be rich today if I had a quarter for every time I heard a woman say, "I wish my husband would grow up." Males generally mature later in life than females, in terms of physical and mental maturity. This may have as much to do with social conditioning as physiological factors. When I was growing up, boys were taught to be physical and active while girls were taught more pragmatic responsibilities such as cooking, sewing, ironing- things that would serve them later in life. Little girls would even receive toys that aided in their development, making their transition to adulthood much smoother than that of young boys. While boys played with guns, bow & arrows, army men, trucks, and

> **At least 86% of males confess to watching animated cartoons well into their twenties.**

cars, girls would play with Easy Bake Ovens, Fashion Plates, doll houses, and kitchen sets. Because they acquired useful domestic skills at much younger ages than boys, girls tended to approach life with a more mature focus. The result is that young males were and still are at a disadvantage when it comes to being domestically and socially responsible.

I wish that I could give young wives some insight as to when their boyish husbands will grow-up, but I don't have predictive powers. Actually, male maturity is a function of the type jobs and responsibilities assumed as young men progress through life. While all people develop and mature differently, men develop in direct proportion to the tasks they take on. See it this way. All boys (by this I also mean men) have latent responsibility built into them, but it takes certain challenges and pressures to draw it out. Consider an interesting statistic. At least 86% of males confess to watching animated cartoons well into their twenties. Of those young men, from the same survey, who confessed to using marijuana while in their twenties, most viewed watching cartoons as a main staple of their daily activity. I am not suggesting that viewing cartoons reveals a lack of maturity. But on the other hand, it doesn't expose a great deal of manhood either.

Maturing would seem to be a more difficult proposition for men than women. Basically, it all comes down to the difference in how parents and society, for that matter, raise boys and girls. Growing up in the same house with little age difference between them will reveal that a sister will quickly begin to outdistance her brother in areas of responsibility by the time the two become teenagers. How can this be when they were raised in the same house by the same parents? Easy, parents continue to perpetuate the same type of gender conditioning that has existed in our cultures for many generations. And it has to do with the expectations parents place on young girls versus that which is placed on young boys. Our daughters are taught to assume responsibility at earlier ages than our sons–responsibilities like cooking, house cleaning and babysitting. While sharp gender distinctions have blurred over the years, they still exist.

Consider how young girls play or should I say train for the future. Girls grow up playing house with their dolls. While playing with their Barbie dolls, they will change diapers, feed, bathe, dress, correct, and groom to meet Ken- all in the same afternoon. Wow! What an awesome way to prepare for future reality. The girls are receiving what I call on-the-job training, while the boys are still playing in the sand box wrestling with their neighborhood friends. The males are often given very little chores while the girls are trained to become Miss little home maker. You see, it's all in the training.

I grew up in a home with all boys and no girls. My female first cousin, whose name will remain anonymous, was the closest I ever came to knowing what having a sister was like. She and her mother lived with my family for a short time. I can recall her getting an Easy Bake Oven for Christmas, and I was completely floored. It fascinated me that she didn't receive a bag of marbles or army men. Her toys were so much more technologically advanced than my toys because hers were small scale versions of real kitchen items. We didn't have remote controlled cars when I was growing up. All my toys required that I use my imagination. Guess what! I soon discovered that I was more interested in eating her real Easy Bake Oven cakes than playing with my pretend armies.

I believe that I was rather fortunate growing up in a house with all boys. Because my mother worked hard all day, she had to train us to assume the role of domestic engineers (today's politically correct euphemism for house cleaners). Ironing clothes, vacuuming, and doing the dishes were part of our responsibilities. No one was exempt from house chores in my family. My mother even taught us to prepare meals- in which one chore I particularly hated. She would use the excuse that one day you are going to be on your own; and you are going to have to know how to cook for yourselves. Yea, right, I thought then. I believe that my mother's training is the main reason why I am so meticulous when it comes to cleaning house.

As a result, I have a deep appreciation for women and the role they have traditionally played in the family. Their contribution to the family is never ending and seldom gets the recognition deserved. I strongly believe in sharing in the household responsibilities. Unlike me, many of my childhood friends would escape to "la la land" and leave all the household chores to their sisters. For this very reason, many young men have a hard time adjusting to adult responsibilities. Most of them are clueless when it comes to doing something as simple as washing clothes; they don't know that you're suppose to separate colors from whites or that there is a difference between a cold-water wash and hot-water washes. Men, if you ever want to upset your wife, wash the jeans, whites and dry clean only clothes in the same load using bleach. I assure you that you may not recover from this mistake for a long time. So, heed this warning.

As I pinpoint some of the factors that plague most troubled marriages, allow me to shed some light on a few issues that many husbands have with their young wives. When a woman is immature and is more interested in talking on the phone all day with her girl friends than with attending to the needs of her home, know that problems are sure to develop. Young wives who are guilty of this kind of neglect rarely comprehend the disservice they do to their families. This situation is particularly troubling in cases where the husband works and the wife is a stay at home mom. The truth of the matter is that it is difficult for any man to want to remain in a marriage where when he comes home from work the baby's diaper needs changing, the house is a mess, and dinner is not prepared. I would be more understanding if the woman also had a job. In this case the household duties should be evenly divided, but if you are at home all day and the house is a mess, get up and clean up.

> *For the first time in our society, women are approaching marriage just as irresponsibly as men because their focus is on careers and not the home.*

If a woman has never been properly trained to run an entire household, she will most likely falter in this area due to feeling overwhelmed. Unfortunately, this appears to be the norm with our many young women today. Because of today's social trends and the frantic pace of life, women are growing up with the same mindset as men when it comes to home front responsibilities. They are just as likely to work outside the home as men. For the first time in our society, women are approaching marriage just as irresponsibly as men because their focus is on careers and not the home. And as a result, no one is left to tend the home.

Many of today's young couples are completely unaware of the full ramifications of getting married without receiving any form of premarital counseling. In most cases, young couples do not want a relationship like their parents had. Consequently, young men and women are approaching marriage without any solid reference points from which to set their own course. The effect is that today's marriage relationships lack the foundation to sustain the lives that rest on them. While our parents were not successful on every front, they did have the essential ingredients in their marriages that enabled them to weather the storms against the family. If the foundation is cracked and unstable, then so will the marriage be.

> *For this reason, you must avoid marrying a boy or girl; instead choose a responsible man or woman.*

A child has no business engaging in the affairs of adults. Today, babies are having babies. And as a result, our high schools have to provide daycare services for its students, which is a testament of this fact. Our tax dollars continue to subsidize symptoms rather than address the real problem. But when children (immature adults) lack the maturity to comprehend the consequences of their actions, they will run away and abandon the fruit of their actions when times get tough. For this reason, you must avoid marrying a boy or girl; instead choose a responsible man or woman.

Jotting Down Things to Remember

Jotting Down Things to Remember

Jotting Down Things to Remember

CHAPTER FOUR

Fixing You Is Draining Me

Humor: A man explained how he and his wife learned to resolve their differences. He said, "I don't try to run her life and I don't try to run mine."

CHAPTER FOUR

Fixing You Is Draining Me

Rarely do I experience marriage situations where husbands are more vocal than their wives. And rarely do I experience counseling sessions or daily encounters with couples where the husband is free to speak without being constantly interrupted by the wife. It has been said that women have the capability to speak two thousand more words a day than most men. I believe that there is some truth to this belief. Typically in my counseling sessions with married couples, I notice that men are at a loss for words, and when this happens, women tend to become irate. Oftentimes, I have to pump the man for information, trying to get him to say what he's really thinking. It really isn't his fault because most men have not been taught to express themselves on a personal level. Unless it pertains to sports, work or business you may not get much else. I am not being critical of the man; I am only highlighting a serious truth concerning the inability or willingness of most men to substantive communication.

Husbands would rather apply quick fixes to their problems rather than to talk about solutions. Wives would rather discuss their problems rather than address fixes. In the woman's mind, problems are solved through active communication. In the husband's mind, talking is a waste of time. To most men, going straight to the heart of the matter is the logical next step, not talking about it. Herein is the root of the problem- two people approaching problem solving from entirely different perspectives. Often, both spouses have this idea that they can fix the problem, when in essence they are secretly trying to fix one another. And frankly, this approach is killing the marriage and putting a strain on their emotional strength.

When communication is the problem, wives do not need a handy man any more than the husband needs a mother.

"You're the problem, not me!" exclaim individuals who focus only on others and seldom on themselves. Not only are these people out of touch with their hearts, but they are also afraid to look within their hearts. They need to keep the focus outward because they are afraid of whom they will see inside. They may find the mean, critical person they claim their spouse to be, when, in actuality, that person is living within. It may be too painful for them to discover that they are not simply a part of the problem, but that they are the problem. Don't put this book down yet; continue reading it and allow it to expose some undesirable characteristics you may be harboring. I am not trying to identify who's at fault for the devastation in the marital relationship; I desire only to eradicate the problem itself.

Part of the root problem that exists within the confines of most marriages is defective self-images. Husbands and wives are human beings who are very strong and yet very fragile. People have been known to overcome some of the most horrific situations imaginable. Yet most married couples seem unwilling to fight through the challenges common to all close-quartered, human interaction, let alone marriage.

Couples are oftentimes breakable, but not perishable. How breakable we are depends largely on the strength of our self-image. When our self-image is unhealthy or has been shattered, we become dangerous to other people. It is potentially very dangerous when individuals enter marriage covenants carrying the baggage of past pains and disappointments. What never gets resolved prior to marriage becomes a part of the relationship after vows are exchanged. When you minimize your self-worth, the value you place on your spouse will always only be horizontal to your own, seldom ever higher. When you hurt, you tend to cause pain to others; when you're happy, you will seek to make others happy as well.

Most marriages can do extremely well if individuals would search their own hearts before being critical of their spouses. Being married doesn't necessarily mean that you truly know your spouse. You don't think like your spouse thinks, but you think they do. In other words, husbands and wives tend to believe they are great mind readers and that they are always tuned into the thoughts of their spouses. As a result, dangerous assumptions are made. STOP SECOND GUESSING YOUR SPOUSE!

If you can shape your spouse into what you want them to become, you should never have married him or her in the first place. I can recall watching a movie called *Jerry McGuire*, played by Tom Cruise. In one scene, Jerry McGuire was standing outside the kitchen, when he over heard two sisters talking about him. One woman, who was his girl friend, was so happy that he stayed with her through the night that she starting dreaming of how she could change him. She said, "I love him for the man he almost is." Wow! Does this mean that she has a lot a work to do? Absolutely! If you feel that you have to fix your spouse, then you married the wrong person. This is one reason why communication is so difficult among couples. One spouse will resent the other partner who feels that they are not good enough the way they are. As a result, one person will soon shut down or tune the other out. I am not suggesting that in marriage individuals shouldn't continually strive to improve themselves as much as possible. On the contrary, but it is not the job of one spouse to fix the other person.

> ***A person should never be defined by someone's image of him or her.***

Individuals should work on their flaws based on love of self first then out of commitment to the other person. How can you truly love others when you don't love yourself? Every person has areas that need improvement. It actually becomes exciting when you are working to better your relationship with your spouse by working on your own idiosyncrasies.

Allow me to designate the areas of effort that should be considered. My reason for doing this is that an unhappy and miserable spouse can impose some very impractical and unreasonable demands on his or her partner. For instance, one woman was terribly dissatisfied with her husband's lack of communication skills. She knew before she married him that he was not strong in the area of verbally expressing himself. Not only did her husband have a slight speech impediment, but he also did not conjugate verbs well. She would belittle him in front of others because she felt embarrassed when he spoke to others at casual functions. She would make apologies for him because she assumed that everyone thought the same way she did about her husband's verbal skills. In actuality, people liked him very much, but they would generally make every effort to avoid her.

He became so uncomfortable in public settings with his wife that he would find reasons not to attend functions to which they were invited. She could not understand why her husband did not want to attend public events with her. One day I said to the woman, "Are you so blind and preoccupied by what you expect out of your husband that you do not realize that you are mainly responsible for his insecurity?" I knew that he loved her, but his self-image was wounded by someone he trusted with a deep-seated insecurity. She would demand that he walk around the house practicing his verbal skills so that he would not embarrass her in public. What is so strange about this situation is that she herself never finished high school. It wasn't as though she held any exalted social standing to justify her proud arrogance, not that one ever could. She had a very lofty image of herself that was based on an over-inflated ego. The way she spoke of her accomplishments, I originally thought that she had earned a Ph. D. in physics or something close to it. She was a high school drop out. I am not saying this to denigrate those who may not have earned their high school diplomas, nor am I suggesting that a college degree makes a person better or more intelligent than a person with only a high school education. But with all her boasting, she had nothing to substantiate why she was so condescending towards her husband.

My first thoughts were to get her husband to talk about how he felt about her perception of him. Needless to say, he answered like most men. He stated that he felt bad about his

When you have a longing to repair a defect in your spouse, it is usually the mirror you're looking at.

wife's feelings of him, but more so about how he simply copes by holding in his anger whenever she demeans him in public. After several minutes of letting him talk, she made quite a few attempts to interrupt him. But I would not permit her to interrupt, as I had to firmly assert his right to continue talking. I asked her to notice her uncontrollable desire to defend her actions while he spoke. He did not speak ill of her, but she obviously thought that how he felt about himself was putting a great deal of pressure on her. She had to come to grips with why he was feeling so disengaged from their marriage. While he focused and spoke of improving himself, she only felt hurt and resentment. She gave me all the evidence I needed to make my point when she said, "I was only trying to help him become a better person." When you have a longing to repair a defect in your spouse, it is usually the mirror you're looking at.

I asked her, "Are you his coach or his wife?" First things first, work on yourself and then you can assist your partner while he is trying to improve himself. It was amazing the things he would do to get his wife's approval. As I continued, I realized that her wall was cracking. It hurts to face your self when for so long you deceived yourself into believing that you were another way. She saw how much her husband really loved her, and her husband discovered how much she did not really love herself. As the tears flowed, I too became emotional, but I knew that I had to press a little harder. Her husband began to pacify her by saying how he was as much to blame as she was. I had to quickly interrupt and show him how he has always cushioned the bottom for her by putting blame on himself. Of course, like most people, she loved having that kind of guilt and condemnation shifted to someone else. But this was one time the tears should and would serve their true purpose.

> *When you truly see what is wrong with yourself, your heart is open to what is truly right.*

Healing like this takes time, and it can be the best time spent because you are finally discovering you. When you learn that while you are trying to fix your spouse, you are actually subconsciously pointing to what you do not like about yourself. It's like standing in an open jail cell. All you have to do is acknowledge what is in front of you and then simply walk through the open doors to freedom. Every person is right in his or her own eyes, but it takes a wise person to acknowledge when he or she is wrong.

It is always taxing when you are trying to change others. I have learned to allow people to simply be who they are or at least who they think they are. Pain hides behind every critical spirit. In most cases, people will avoid every situation that can cause their pain to resurface. People are generally unhappy with themselves for many reasons. Unhappy people create an ambience of unhappiness. When a marriage has gone bad, it is because a couple has a warped concept of their obligation to each other. Husbands and wives are obligated to surrender to one another and make the other person the priority and not self. It is not the marriage that needs fixing; it is the people inside the marriage who need to be fixed.

Husband, your wife did not marry you for you to work on her, and vice versa. You married one another because you loved each other, and you recognized a void that the person could potentially fill. If you are strong in every area of life, you do not need a spouse. Moreover, you were not constructed to be strong in every area of life. Your spouse becomes your strength in areas where you're susceptible. Every doctor needs a nurse; every lawyer hires a legal assistant; every President has a Vice President; and every husband has a wife. You are to fulfill life's purpose by performing in your god-given role. Humans are uniquely joined together on this planet, and we must interact with each other in order to discover to whom we are assigned. I am a better man today because of my wife. Oftentimes, my wife just lies in the bed and laughs when I reminisce about when I used to play sports. It doesn't cause her to think any better or worse of me. That's what I like about her. She learned early in our marriage that it can be taken quite defensively if she points a finger at my Achilles' heel. I also learned that if my wife's weaknesses are my strengths, then she has no weaknesses because I cover them. If I nit-pick at her weakness, I am compounding her frustration and making life miserable for the both of us.

Your weakness becomes your greatest asset because this is where your spouse is at his or her greater good.

Learn to not be critical of one another. Choose rather to become sympathetic and understanding, knowing that where you are weak, your spouse is proportionately strong in that area. Your weakness becomes your greatest asset because this is where your spouse is at his or her greater good. Husbands and wives, over time, should learn to compliment one another and not analyze and critique each other. This is the age old problem that plagues most married couples. As one corrects the other, the recipient of the correction receives it as a rebuke and counters the correction by broadcasting his or her own criticisms. This type of back and forth banter not only weakens the cords that bind the marriage, but it also displays a lack of respect as well. Every complaint, although true, isn't always necessary to voice. Wait, be calm, and then discuss the issue as intelligent, mature adults. The proper approach to any situation can be the difference between night and day. Think about what you are thinking about. Consider how you would like to be considered by your spouse concerning an issue, and then keep it on the canvas of your heart so that you will do to others what you would like done to you.

The Secret Motive to Repair

You are of better service to your spouse with your arms embracing rather than your fingers pointing.

Some mal-formed pattern in our thinking has led to the belief that fixing others should be done by showing them where they are wrong. Usually, what we consider as character flaws in others is what we despise about ourselves. What gets under our skin most is how others react in certain situations that is so foreign from how we would have responded in those same circumstances. If, for example, the husband doesn't wash the clothes in the same manner as the wife, one person will invariably view the other person's method as wrong or inferior. Washing colors first or whites first is not a cardinal sin. In either case, the clothes are getting washed. This attitude comes from a self-righteous attitude that derives from one person feeling that his way or her way is the only logical way to perform a particular chore. Arguing over such pettiness has led to more failed marriages than you might care to imagine. The bible reveals that it is the little foxes that destroy the vine, meaning that small, trivial problems are often the root cause of the destruction of great structures.

The way you really help your spouse is by first correcting yourself. We must come to grips with fixing ourselves if we want to benefit others. It is not only impossible, but absurd to attempt to help someone while judging them at the same time. When you are blinded by the need to judge others, you disqualify yourself from being able to help them. How can the Prosecutor prosecute the defendant and sit in the jury box as well? You can't prove a person wrong and then give them hope for the future when you also, as the jury, decide the verdict. To be in the best

It is not fatal to accept criticism, but it can prove to be lethal to accept judgment.

position to render aid to your spouse, you must become the person who binds the wounds when the other person is hurt. And this you can only do by readjusting the role you are to play where your spouse in concerned. You are of better service to your spouse with your arms embracing rather than your fingers pointing.

Examine yourself to find the real reason why you feel as though you cannot accept your spouse the way they are. It is not fatal to accept criticism, but it can prove to be lethal to accept judgment. You must personally recognize that you may have a problem with an inner need to judge others. Once you reach this conclusion, you are then in position to begin the process of improving yourself rather than constantly trying to be approved by others. Learn to be completely honest with yourself. It is essential to purging oneself of toxic attitudes that stem from a heart of insecurity and perhaps self-hatred.

How Can I Change Me?

*You can change,
if you are willing to change.*

Let's get some things straight. All of us, at one time or another has judged others unfairly. We've passed on information about other people to others that we did not personally know to be true or not. Consider the source before you pass on any damaging information about others. You can change, if you are willing to change. The entire idea of relating to people on the basis of unwarranted judgment removes us from the realm of reality, responsibility, and integrity. It is actually easier to help and improve yourself than it is to try and help or improve your spouse. How does the mind of a critical person operate? It works similar to a person who is over weight by fifty pounds attempting to motivate a person over weight by only twenty pounds to lose weight. The person who is fifty pounds over weight may pretend to be content with his or her condition and express no desire to lose weight. But this can be the same person to project his or her deep-seated insecurities onto the person that he or she is trying to help by making snide or derogatory comments. Accepting the truth about yourself can be emotionally painful and taxing when you have ignored it for many years.

Ask God for the inner strength to acknowledge your own shortcomings and inadequacies. Be strong and fair when dealing with your personal insecurities. Refuse to become lenient and soft on your insecurities. But at the same time, you must not beat yourself up about what you can change. Confess to your spouse the negative and unfair assessments that you harbor where he or she is concerned, and then ask for their forgiveness. Do not be afraid to expose your hidden need to be manipulative. Dig deeper to discover why. You may feel that manipulation keeps you in the driver's seat and indirectly in control of your spouse's weakness.

Learn to confess without duress and you'll find your marriage truly blessed.

Admit to your spouse if you have compiled a list of his or her negative qualities that you are quickly able to draw upon as ammunition to use whenever you feel the need to control or belittle the individual. Remember! Your marriage is not a war, it is a love affair.

Jotting Down Things to Remember

Jotting Down Things to Remember

Jotting Down Things to Remember

CHAPTER FIVE

For Troubled Marriages

*Where rules exist,
discipline is inevitable.*
-- Mikel Brown

CHAPTER FIVE

For Troubled Marriages

It takes time to produce a good marriage; it takes longer, however, to turn a troubled marriage into a good marriage. In order to make your marriage work, you must stop doing what does not work. There is nothing in a troubled marriage that cannot be fixed with a little help. And using a hammer to solve certain problems will only shatter the marriage into tiny little pieces. Usually it is not the marriage that needs fixing; it is the hearts and minds of the people in it that need repair. The institution of marriage is perfect, but it is comprised of imperfect people who try to manipulate rules to accommodate their notions of what they believe marriage is. All sporting events are established according to clearly established rules and regulations to maintain order and prescribe boundaries of play. This is the reason such competition is considered an organized sport. Without governing rules to maintain order, anarchy and lawlessness will become the established order. Where rules exist, discipline is inevitable.

Every professional athlete realizes that in order to be successful at a particular sport, he or she must first learn the rules that govern his or her profession and then submit to a regimen that will enable him or her to compete physically at that level. If athletes do not abide by the rules of the game, they disqualify themselves from competition. We live in a society where rules and laws are necessary in order to govern the affairs of people. Laws are established to protect the people, but on occasion they become so twisted as to offer more protection to the guilty. The United States Judicial system has no real clearly defined absolutes. As a result, many conclude that rules are meant to be broken and boundaries are there to be crossed. Thus, where our laws are nebulous or obscure, the people cannot properly be governed. My intent is not to give the reader a lesson on the purpose of law, but to merely establish a basis for why things often go awry in any institutional structure.

The marriage system will stand firm by itself, but the couple will crack under the weight of their ignorance.

Just as rules apply to the functioning of governmental institutions, so too do they apply to the functioning of marriage. Different sets of rules govern different types of games. And what adequately controls one sport would permit chaos if applied to another. In order for a couple to experience a successful marriage, the individuals must be willing to learn and abide by the rules set forth to govern marriage. I am not suggesting that marriage is a game. I merely wish to use sports as an analogy for the sake of facilitating an understanding. Marriage can work just fine if you are willing to work properly within the system. Unselfishness is one of the rules that promote harmony between couples. When this particular principle is violated, marriage will cease to serve the parties as intended, and the violation may cause them to be ejected from the game, so to speak. In other words, the marriage system will eject the couple just as our bodies regurgitate bad food when it is consumed. Marriage is not intended to work in the presence of the toxic pollutants we introduce to it- pollutants such as anger, selfishness, bitterness, etc. The marriage system will stand firmly despite our poor execution, but the couple will crack under the weight of their ignorance. You cannot have a troubled marriage without first having troubled people. People tend to bring into their marriages the baggage of unresolved personal issues. Many of our insecurities and hurts are never properly dealt with prior to marriage, if at all. And oftentimes individuals explode as a result of frustration with their partners and conclude that the marriage isn't working. When in fact, it is not that the marriage is not working; it is that the people in it have failed to abide by its rules.

Trouble within a marriage does not signal that it is beyond repair. The marriage can turn out just fine if the couple will simply make some minor adjustments. The first thing that must happen in order to fix a trouble relationship is that one or both individuals must cease in their efforts to fix the other person. 99.9% of all problems in a marital relationship are as a result of hypocrisy. By this I am referring to those instances where one spouse is able to articulate what they feel is seriously wrong with the other person, but they are at a loss for words when it comes to identifying their own shortcomings. People are finger pointers by nature, and we are always quick to recognize when someone else is at fault.

After partaking of the forbidden tree, Adam was at a loss when God began to press him for answers regarding his condition of disobedience. Rather than take responsibility for his actions, Adam said, "The woman you gave me caused me to eat from the tree." Ever since that day, all of humanity has had to pay the price for this one disgraceful act of treason against God. Understand that the problem was not with the Garden of Eden; it was a perfect place. The problem resulted when Adam and Eve chose to disregard a clear command from their creator. Consequently, they were both expelled from the garden. After Adam and Eve had sinned in the Garden, they saw each other's nakedness through judgmental eyes. What they once saw as beautiful and innocent before their fall, was suddenly given a name after the fall called, "Naked." Their spiritual sight was removed and replaced with critical, fault-finding eyesight. It was from this point on that husband and wife have become self-appointed judges. Without anyone else to judge their actions, they decided to judge one another.

If the husband feels he's right and if the wife feels she's right, who then is wrong? If couples do not have each other to blame, on whom do they blame their failure? Here lies the problem; the couple is the problem. The irony of it is that disputing couples cannot see that the marriage is not the problem. The marriage institution is completely blameless. When couples divorce, why do we insinuate that the marriage has gone sour? Let's face it! You cannot have a

***The marriage institution
is completely blameless.***

troubled marriage without troubled people. If the individuals would commit to restructuring their thought patterns concerning marriage and each another, then marriages would flow smoothly.

People normally bring excess baggage into their relationships, and usually this baggage is not noticed until after each person has said, "I do." Once "I do" is declared, all the excess cargo is dragged out of the closet and into the foreground of the relationship. As they begin to unpack, you will discover problems and bad habits that trace all the way back to their toddler years. In such case, most couples are without the tools to remedy their predicament, unless one of the two is a psychiatrist. We must begin the quest for solutions by dealing with what is at the core of troubled individuals. Then the journey to reclaim a healthy marriage can begin. For this reason, I am a strong advocate of pre-marital counseling. When people are courting, rarely will the partners get to see the real person. During the dating period, people are on their best behavior because they do not want to risk losing their potential partner. There are steps and a checklist that I recommend for candidates who are serious about screening their potential spouses for compatibility. By guiding your prospective spouse through the following questionnaire, you will gain great insights into whether that individual is right for you. The individual does not even need to know that he or she is being interviewed.

**Whatever is in the root
is in the fruit.**

Write down the numbers 1 through 10. One is the least favorable and 10 is the best rating possible. The number six will be an average number and any rating 5 and below will indicate serious problems that will surface later, if you choose to marry the individual.

(1) What kind of relationship did you have with your

parents?
(2) Are your parents divorced?
(3) How long have your parents been married?
(4) How long have your parents been divorced?
(5) How did you handle your parents being divorced?
(6) Do you hold any resentment towards any of your parents?
(7) Do you feel your parents expressed their love toward you?
(8) Were any of your parents abusive with their spouse?
(9) Were your parents verbally or physically abusive with you?
(10) Have you ever been raped or molested?
(11) Did any of your siblings force you to perform oral sex or such thing?
(12) Are you happy with yourself or generally dissatisfied with your life?

How you rate the person's answers will reveal how healthy the relationship was between your potential spouse and his or her parents. Knowing the type of relationship your future spouse had with his or her parents suggests plenty about the kind of relationship you will have with that individual. If the person had an unhealthy relationship with his or her parents, the after effects could very well spill over onto you and your children. Your tactful inquiring of his or her parents serves just as important a purpose for you as their questioning you does for them. What you can learn about the parents can give you insight into the life of their son or daughter. Why is this so important? As you know, genetics are passed on to the children from the parents. Therefore, whatever is in the root is in the fruit. Now this is not to suggest that there cannot be variations in the personality or that the children cannot have an entirely different disposition. In the overall scheme of genetics, some negative and or positive attributes can be passed on. For instance, the likelihood for spousal abuse is much higher for those persons who have experienced it between their mother and father. Spousal abuse is an epidemic in America and the percentage is only increasing.

I have counseled both men and women who have experienced spousal abuse. Of course, the percentage of abuse is much higher among women. I have viewed at times sons becoming verbally abusive with their mothers because they emulated their fathers' abusive behavior toward those same women. Despite my efforts in this particular chapter to alert people to this epidemic, I'm afraid that my cries will go unheeded by many who will read this book. In some cases, physical abuse started during the dating stage and the abused individuals ignored every sign that their relationship was going to be a rocky one. There is also an increase of physical abuse among dating and sexually active high school students. A person should never hesitate to remove oneself from an abusive relationship because one's life may very well depend upon it. The cry I hear most after a woman has been victimized is, "I made him angry! He's normally a gentle and loving person. He loves me and I love him. It will all work out." If a woman chooses to remain in an abusive relationship without demanding that her husband seek professional help, she risks not only her life, but also the lives of her children and anyone who seeks to help her.

One case of abuse was so horrible I couldn't believe what I was hearing. The wife was eight months pregnant at the time she experienced a brutal attack by her husband. Her husband had been abusive before, but this event seemed to be the straw that broke the camel's back. The husband returned home from work and everything seemed to be going fine

For Troubled Marriages

until he could not find his pack of cigarettes. After screaming at his wife for moving his pack of cigarettes, he began to beat her in the face with a closed fist. He kicked her in the stomach and hit her so hard that he knocked her through the bathroom door. She fell to the ground, hit her head and was unconscious for an unspecified amount of time. When she regained consciousness, her husband was still beating her. I know how horrible this must seem as you read this account, but these types of cases are very real and too numerous to count. I am certain you have heard of worse cases than this one. Fortunately for this woman, her baby survived, but her marriage did not.

A person should never hesitate to remove oneself from an abusive relationship because one's life may very well depend upon it.

In all my years of premarital and marriage counseling, there are a few cases that stand out from all the others. This one couple, in particular, seemed destined for ruin from the start. When they came to my office, they were both in their early twenties. He was in the military and she also held down a job. They were always arguing and fighting about petty things. They had all the signs of a troubled marriage. He drank often, and she liked to party. This combination doesn't work well in any marriage for it breeds both infidelity and abusiveness. They wanted help, so they agreed to counseling. I only worked with them for about three sessions over a very short period of time. Three sessions of marital counseling is not going to resolve all the years of being mis-educated. Effective counseling must deal with the deprogramming and reprogramming of information. Proper work on the marriage means that the couple must first work on themselves. As I continued to counsel this young couple and give them home assignments, they seemed to make steady progress. I learned that in their childish stupidity they would often fight using shoes and knives as weapons. They were both very abusive towards each other, but the man was usually the instigator. Please understand me when I say that she was not at all innocent in this saga. Stupidity coupled with drugs and alcohol will certainly lead to abusive behavior.

During my third counseling session with them, they admitted to having some small arguments, but they were able to quickly gain control of the situation. For some strange reason, I really liked this couple. They had the kind of personalities that just grows on a person. They were young and inexperienced in life. Both of them lacked safe and loving environments growing up and both were exposed to many of the ills of street life. I recall seeing them outside my office waiting for marriage counseling. When I saw them together, they appeared to be so happy. Then the unspeakable happened a few days later. I received a call that the young husband was dead. I could hardly believe what I was hearing. I said to the caller, "Stop kidding with me!" The seriousness of the caller's voice indicated that this was no joke. Since I was the counselor of record with this young couple, I was allowed to talk with the wife who was accused of the murder and who was in the custody of the Military Police. Since the counseling sessions were private, I could not divulge too much information. I was bewildered as to what could have happened to make her kill her husband. No one knew exactly what had happened because the woman was too hysterical to offer any clear answers. They approached this case as a domestic abuse situation; therefore, they brought in a female counselor and a doctor to examine her. After a thorough exterior examination, they discovered bruises on her body that suggested physical abuse as the possible motive. But the officials could not get her to talk much to confirm their suspicions. Because the young woman requested my presence, I was summoned to the hospital where she was being questioned and examined by the female counselor and the doctor. After I had arrived and was escorted into the examining room, she ran to me and gave me an overwhelmingly strong embrace, as if to suggest she felt comforted by my presence. I guess, somewhat, that she and her husband had grown fond of me and began to regard me as their mentor. They had no family living where they were stationed in the military, and perhaps they gravitated to me because I represented the next closest thing to family where they were concerned. I was asked by the female counselor to get her to talk, and as I spoke words of comfort to her, her hysteria began to subside.

I spoke casually to her so that she would not feel threatened or intimidated. As we talked, I asked her, "What started the confrontation between you and your husband?" She claimed that he had been drinking and returned home and became physically abusive. "He kept pushing me and then slapped me," she said. She thought perhaps he was playing until he slapped her. When he came home she was in the kitchen preparing a meal. She yelled for him to stop hitting her, but he continued to grab at her while she was trying to get away. She picked up a knife in the kitchen and informed him several times to leave her along. As she held the knife in her hand, he reached for her waist to keep her from swinging it at him. As she fought to release her hand, he for some reason let her go. The sudden release of her waist caused her arm to come down with such force that she cut him deep enough to sever the main artery to the heart. He bled to death on the kitchen floor, dying in only a matter of minutes.

To say the least, I was disturbed in my heart and very saddened by this senseless tragedy. I really don't know what else could have been done on my part to prevent what happened other than living with them round the clock to ensure that they were actually applying the principles I had been teaching them. But I know that this was not an option. Could this incident have been avoided? Yes! Emphatically! The symptoms are secondary when you are having marital problems. If a couple can avoid exaggerating the minor issues and focus on correcting the major ones, they will make it through every storm.

> ***Don't avoid the hard and embarrassing issues because they can save your relationship.***

Don't avoid the hard and embarrassing issues because they can save your relationship. You are not at war with each other, you are married. You are aware of most of your spouse's weaknesses and strengths, but this information is not ammunition to be used against your partner, but tools rather to help you serve and relate to them. The marriage bond will only strengthen as your weaknesses become your greatest asset with the person you love. The next chapter should be read by every person who is considering marriage, currently married, divorced or widowed. My next chapter holds many of the secrets to overcoming any negative condition that might exist within a marriage.

Jotting Down Things to Remember

Jotting Down Things to Remember

CHAPTER SIX

Successfully Overcoming The Pain of An Affair

Controlling your emotions during the pain of infidelity is the key to avoiding the suffering of it. Pain is inevitable but suffering is optional.
-- Mikel Brown

CHAPTER SIX

Successfully Overcoming The Pain of an Affair

This is a very sensitive subject because the hurt experienced, as a result of betrayal, is just as painful as that caused by a stabbing or gun shot. I have helped many couples deal with the pain of infidelity. This type of pain, however, can never be fixed or repaired with surgery. Instead, the pain caused when one partner goes outside the marriage for sexual intimacy can only be healed through the process of love, patience, decisiveness and forgiveness. Let's face it, infidelity is an epidemic in this nation, and it doesn't seem as though the numbers are going to recede anytime soon. There are no ready made, step-by-step quick solutions individuals can turn to for answers when infidelity knocks on the door of a relationship. The mixed emotions that victims of affairs go through are horrendous. One day a person can feel completely helpless and fall apart; while the next day that individual can feel revengeful. One's emotions can become totally uncontrollable, and negative thoughts become inescapable. Controlling your emotions during the pain of infidelity is the key to avoiding the suffering of it. Pain is inevitable; suffering is optional. I am not going to try to convince you that overcoming such a challenge is easy, but it is possible. Balance must be maintained through the entire ordeal if the couple agrees to continue in marriage.

Allow me to outline the steps that I have followed for years–steps which have helped restore hope and love to broken relationships. These steps are fail-proof. If a couple is willing to comply with these steps, their marriage will improve considerably. Some of the steps may seem unfair at times, but I assure you that they are very fair. I have invested many years of time and energy into public and private marital sessions and have done a great deal of personal study all to help couples, not simply cope with the pain of adultery, but eradicate it all together. What person is interested in staying in a marriage where the painful memory of a partner's treachery is ever-present? I believe that I can help break that unwanted link to the pain of the past and help you to experience the freedom and power of forgiveness.

The four steps are exclusively for people who have experienced the hurt of betrayal firsthand because they are the ones who must now battle through feelings of severe low self-esteem. So, let's get this session started and get your marriage back on the right road. Even if your marriage started off shaky, allow the shaking to rattle everything off until nothing unstable remains. Far better to work with what is properly and firmly attached to the relationship than to fight to patch and preserve what does not benefit the marriage. If you don't already have a trusted pastor or professional counselor to help referee some of your sessions, find one. A highly trained neutral party serves to maintain order and help keep your mind full of positive input.

***Step 1*–Fight the mental stress that can cause indecisiveness.**

After the initial shock of discovering that your spouse had an affair, make no decisions about your marriage until you have thoroughly thought things through. After you have prayed and cried, cried and prayed; refuse to lose control of your emotions. Learning to control your emotions is very important at this stage. I am not suggesting at all that you should begin re-channeling your emotions; rather allowing yourself to discover what God has placed in you. It is quite natural to feel hurt, pain, anger, frustration and yes even love. Unless you are from another planet, you will go through a wide range of emotions and moods, but do not allow them to become uncontrollable.

Once you are able to gain some sense of control over your emotions, you can now begin to assess whether or not you would like to continue in your marriage. Biblically, legally and morally, you do have grounds for divorce. Many Christians seem to wrestle with the issue of divorce after infidelity has occurred. Adultery is a perfectly legitimate reason for divorce, from God's standpoint. Understand that divorce is one of your viable options. Once you are fully aware of what the Bible has to say on this particular issue, you must then make certain decisions regarding the status of your marriage. This needs to be carefully weighed because if you decide to remain in the relationship and your spouse concurs, you are then bound by that decision. If you decide later to divorce, you then have no biblical basis to do so because you can no longer use as a reason the adultery that you are supposed to have forgiven.

I am not advocating divorce as the solution to marital infidelity. I simply want you to be aware of this one option because so many people wrestle with making such a decision, wondering whether or not they are doing the right thing. Even God gives us a way out of our marriages in cases of infidelity because He too knows firsthand the pain of an unfaithful spouse (the children of Israel). No one should be allowed to help you make such an important decision, other than God. Because this decision will affect the rest of your life, you need to consider God for answers. Since He is omniscient, He will help you with the implications of divorce if you seek His guidance.

I have informed people of their right to divorce if they no longer desire to remain married. And at times both spouses thought that I was trying to separate the two of them. On the contrary, my aim is to bring the injured party into the reality of how his or her choice will impact many other lives, namely children. Should children be considered before making such a decision? No! The children aren't married to your spouse; you are. Did your spouse take the children into consideration before committing adultery? It is important that you do not allow others to project their concerns onto you.

You must also consider whether the unfaithful spouse desires to remain in the marriage. If the person is willing to continue the marriage, consider also whether children are involved or whether the unfaithful spouse is still romantically connected to the other person. These probing questions will be the source of tremendous mental attack that you will, no doubt, experience on the road to healing. For this reason, it is vitally important that you make a conscious decision about your life and the future of your marriage. All these things must be carefully considered because if you decide to remain in the marriage, you will know, to some degree, what you will be up against in the future. You will have to fight off very troubling and tormenting mental thoughts. And at times, you will feel compelled to monitor your spouse's every move because of the resultant loss of trust. You may even entertain thoughts of revenge, carefully crafting plots to indulge in your own extra-marital fling. Relying on God will help you to get through this very troubling time, and He will even give you reasons to believe in your marriage again.

Step 2 – Talk and listen patiently to the guilty spouse about what led to the affair.

At one time or another, you are going to have to communicate your feelings and thoughts and hear the feelings and thoughts of your spouse. Getting to the point where the two of you can talk without anger can prove to be valuable in helping you make a good decision. Listen carefully and patiently, but do not accept it when the guilty party tries to downplay the significance of his or her infidelity by stating that the affair was nothing but meaningless sex. This type of response is childish and highlights an unwillingness to own up to one's poor decision making. If the shoe were on the other foot, I wonder whether those same individuals would buy into such lame excuses. I'm certain they would not. When adultery occurs in a marital relationship, that most sacred of intimacies between a husband and wife has been shared with someone outside their covenant.

Don't ask your spouse to share the sordid details of the sexual affair. Knowing the details will serve no meaningful purpose, and you will only become more upset by what you learn of the encounter. In counseling sessions, husbands have asked their wives whether they performed oral sex on the other man; and wives wanted to know all sorts of equally intimate details regarding their husbands' sexual exploits with the other woman. This line of questioning leads to further humiliation and it may even promote a need to compete with the person who stole your spouse's affection. I cannot over-emphasize enough the fact that no individual in a marriage relationship should ever feel as though he or she has to compete for the love and attention of a spouse. Resist the need to know details about their sexual escapades. The important thing is that you know about the affair, and that should be good enough.

Here is some added advice when communicating with your spouse about the affair. Resist the desire to ask the question, "Why?" Can you recall times when you asked your children why they did certain things- things that were so senseless that they defied all logic and reason? Or can you even remember, as a child yourself, your parents asking you that same question? You watched as your children got that dazed and faraway look in their eyes as they began to explore the unknown possibilities of their answers. Even so, what kind of answer are you expecting from your spouse by wanting to know the why for his or her unfaithfulness. Save yourself the frustration of seeing your spouse probe for lame excuses. Without realizing it, you are saying to them, "What you do doesn't really matter as long as your reason can justify the act." If children feel that they can give good enough reasons to justify their behavior, then they will try to get away with murder. Don't ask why!

Step 3– **Do not assemble an unrealistic list of concessions for your spouse to perform.**

I realize that people will always become angry after discovering that a spouse has had an affair. Becoming angry is perfectly natural, but individuals must not become bitter or respond by having a spouse jump through hoops to prove their remorse. Once the guilty party has voiced the desire to hold onto the marriage, the couple should then discuss and agree to certain terms. After the initial pain and pressure of most affairs begins to subside, the guilty individual may begin to feel as though the injured spouse's demands are too unreasonable. But this is the time when the injured party should place demands on the unfaithful spouse that require certain accountability. The demands must be reasonable, and the guilty person must commit to following through with all of them.

Counseling should be one of the first things placed on the list of demands. The person who committed the affair has some internal character flaws that must be addressed; counseling would serve to identify those internal failings that would cause someone to commit adultery. Some years ago, I counseled two individuals who had suffered tremendous devastation as a result of the husband's cheating. During my sessions with the couple, it was discovered that he had a series of adulterous encounters. His wife was passive, but not naïve. He would often berate her publicly. At times she would make attempts to stand up to his disrespect, but she always returned to her passive disposition. It was sad to see the condition of their marriage, but there was nothing I could do about it because she tolerated it. He yelled in one particular counseling session, "I wouldn't have had these affairs if you would simply do what I ask when we are having sex." She cried and said, "You know that I don't feel comfortable doing those things." He did apologize to his wife after I had confronted him about his outburst. I can only imagine how many times he must have said those words to her. I told these two individuals that counseling would not benefit them because she was too tolerant of his cheating. I went on to state that as long as she chose to buy into his erroneous reasons for straying outside the marriage for sexual satisfaction, he would continue to cheat on her. Her failure to stand against this blatant disrespect only fueled his inappropriate behavior.

How can you help a woman deal with an unfaithful spouse when she believes that men are genetically predisposed to having extra-marital affairs. This belief is, no doubt, the result of a great deal of social and cultural conditioning. Many women hold the belief that cheating is what men do, so what can you do about it. Despite the poor examples you may have seen growing up, you must never tacitly encourage your husband to violate his marriage vows by remaining silent to his cheating. You must hold your husband to a higher standard than perhaps your mother did with your father. The fact that many men do cheat on their wives should provide no consolation if you find yourself in a relationship with an unfaithful spouse.

One of the counseling stipulations should be that the counselor must speak alone with the person who committed the adultery. This would increase the likelihood of getting to the actual root of why one spouse feels the need to go outside the relationship for sexual fulfillment. The one-on-one session must never focus on the symptoms of infidelity, but it must seek to identify root causes. Believe it or not, we can trace all of human actions to some root cause. Addressing the root will provide remedy to the rest of the body and ultimately to relationships with others.

***Step 4*–Ask God to help you to release your anger and mistrust.**

The release of anger will result in the destruction of its root cause.

You are no different from anyone else in this world. You feel pain, and your emotions cause you to respond to pain in many different ways. You cry, get angry, and experience mental anguish- all testament to the fact that you are human. I have dealt with people who have experienced every emotion humanly possible after discovering that their spouse had been unfaithful. And yes, murder was even considered, but never carried out. Thank God!

The desire not to want the guilty party to get off without punishment is the primary reason that victims of marital unfaithfulness aren't so readily willing to forgive. And if you have ever experienced tremendous pain caused by another, you know that letting that person off lightly is the furthest thing from your mind. In reality, forgiveness does as much to free you as it does the perpetrator of your hurt. Forgiving your spouse of his or her trespass empowers you and prevents your spouse's sins to gain control over your life. I have seen women lose their hair, men stalk their wives, and people experience devastating mental breakdowns as a result of infidelity. I hope you see just how important it is to release your anger through the healing power of forgiveness. If you don't forgive, your body may eventually succumb to the unhealthy effects that anger and bitterness produce. It is important that you maintain your composure and not fall apart. If you do, your spouse may unwisely conclude that he or she has the upper hand and thus continue in his or her ways.

If your spouse tries to project his or her weaknesses and bad choices onto you, refuse the package and return it to sender.

Don't allow yourself to wear their imperfections. You are not the guilty one, and you should not allow them to make you feel as though you are. If your spouse tries to project his or her weaknesses and bad choices onto you, refuse the package and return it to sender. I have heard many men and women over my many years of counseling say, "Maybe if I had been a better husband or wife and paid attention to their needs." Hogwash! You cannot do more for others than they are willing to do for themselves. We can no more force people to have an affair than we can compel them to love us. This is not the time for pointing fingers, but a time for embracing change. The release of anger will result in the destruction of its root cause.

Step 5–Stop allowing the past to become a continual part of your future.

> *Trying to forget the past doesn't heal the pain nor does it change the past.*

This principle applies to both individuals in the marriage. It is impossible to take the necessary steps toward healing if your focus is only on the pain of the past. Once the two of you commit to making your marriage work, the past must no longer remain an issue. Trying to forget the past doesn't heal the pain nor does it change the past. I know that people like to say that you must forget the past to deal with hurt and disappointment. But in truth, it is easier said than done. You can no more forget the past than you can your own name. Your past is part of you, but not ahead of you.

Most adults experienced cuts and bruises as children, and many of us continue to wear the scars to prove it. When you look at the scars on your body, you don't start to cry when you think about what caused them. Remembering what caused the scars produces no present pain, only memories.

Therefore, it is alright to remember the past, but, it is essential to forget the pain associated with the past. Forgetting the past is impossible unless you have Alzheimer's disease. Trying to forget the past will only leave you with unresolved issues that linger in the back of your mind. The pain that continues to surface with the thought of the past is an indication that you have never completely resolved the issue. Pain is associated with a source. In this case, the source is the infidelity. Sometimes, even the guilty individuals can put themselves through ridiculous demands because of the guilt of hurting their spouse. They will practically do anything in an attempt to make things right without realizing that past wrongs cannot be corrected. The present is all we have with which to work, and it determines our future. Jumping through hoops after an affair will help no one. Being open and dealing with the betrayal will help the injured spouse tremendously. I assure you that beating yourself up and crawling on your bare knees up the Mountain of Guadalupe will only cause you tremendous physical pain and emotional bitterness; because you will soon discover that your attempt to prove your sincerity will not ease the emotional pain of the one you betrayed. Only through your sincere display of love, patience and affirmation can you truly help mend your hurt partner.

Jotting Down Things to Remember

Jotting Down Things to Remember

CHAPTER SEVEN

For Financially Challenged Marriages

*Couples don't necessarily have financial problems;
they have discipline problems.*
   -- Mikel Brown

CHAPTER SEVEN

For Financially Challenged Marriages

Joke: A wife one day asked her husband what he thought of her having plastic surgery. His reply was, "I support that procedure 100%; I think it will help tremendously." So he cut up all of her credit cards.

Two financially ignorant people in a relationship equates to a couple deeply in debt. Ignorance is not necessarily a derogatory word. In its simplest terms, it means to ignore truth or knowledge. Is it such a bad thing to be ignorant? No! But it is a bad thing to stay ignorant. One of the top three reasons for divorce or anxiety in marriage is the mismanagement of money. Statistics show that finances rank among the top causes of divorce, right along with lack of sexual fulfillment and poor communication. I disagree! Neither money, nor sex, nor communication leads to divorce but ignorance and immaturity regarding those areas. Money is not inherently evil. It has no super powers or ability to make anyone do anything against his or her will. In actuality, money is powerless. In my book *"Building Wealth from the Ground Up"*, I go into detail about the perceived value of money, and this book has been instrumental in helping people to better understand how money works.

Our world is governed by the principle of "cause and effect in which it dramatically affects people." Nothing happens without a root cause. God is the cause of all things, but God Himself is uncaused. Everything else is simply a reaction to a previous action. When a couple is experiencing financial difficulty, it is usually as a result of overspending or the mismanagement of the family funds. Conversely, some people fall into financial ruin through circumstances beyond their control, such as a sickness, job loss, or even the death of the primary breadwinner. Others may experience financial pitfalls due to plain neglect. Couples don't necessarily have financial problems; they have discipline problems. Let's get a few things straight. Money is important, and how you handle it is vital to the success of your family's future. If you don't grasp the gravity of this statement, you may very well be traveling in retrograde motion as far as your family's financial progress is concerned.

The lack of money can produce tremendous emotional heartache, and it has also been known to cause ulcers, migraine headaches and a host of other physical ailments. When people say that they do not have money to address life's basic necessities, understand that they have deeper issues to address that exist below the surface of their obvious money shortage. The lack of money is a symptom, not the cause. Most people are not prepared to hear the truth when it comes to their financial predicaments. They like to live in fantasy worlds where the devil can be blamed for every financial woe imaginable. As the comedian Flip Wilson used to say, "The devil made me do it." Unfortunately, many people are quick to blame others for their financial plight. In order to begin putting your finances on the right track, you must begin by acknowledging your shortcomings in this particular area.

> *A good steward of money is a responsible steward despite the amount.*

Many couples experience financial instability because they create new debt whenever they experience a small amount of debt relief as a result of successfully fulfilling a contract obligation. They regard the freed up capital as an occasion to celebrate by purchasing another large ticket item on time. A willful return to the bondage of debt, once freed, is a clear indication that a couple is not serious about financial freedom, especially in cases where the burden of debt nearly tore the family asunder. In such instances, individuals are simply deceiving themselves, knowing they've made no long term commitment to an entirely new lifestyle; one where debt is unwelcome. Cigarette smokers understand this scenario all too well. Many are able to commit to discontinue smoking for a few weeks or months, only to return to their old ways when the call of nicotine becomes too great. To these individuals, quitting for a few months provides enough reassurance that they can quit for good whenever they want to. Couples that experience intermittent freedom from debt, only to return, are also lulled into a false sense of security about their ability to walk away entirely from debt addiction whenever they so choose.

Why do most people immediately conclude that their financial problems are caused due to the lack of money? The first thing many couples do after blaming each other for the financial woes is to begin working overtime and applying for extra jobs. The last thing that these individuals ever do is to seek financial counseling because of its intrusive nature and also because of the regimentation involved with commitment to a spending plan. I would be incredibly rich today if I had a dollar for every time a couple said to me, "I can't understand why we can't seem to get ahead financially. We make more money than ever before, and I even work extra hours to pay off my bills. Why can't I ever seem to get out of debt?"

People who are financially strapped spend so much time trying to correct symptoms that they remain completely oblivious to the root causes of their problems. Working overtime and getting an extra job will no more remedy their financial condition than giving them a million dollars. Jesus taught the disciples an important principle that proves this very point. In the 16th chapter of the book of Luke, he stated, "He who is faithful in least is faithful in much." A good steward of money is a responsible steward despite the amount. I will go even further to suggest that money is not the solution to the lack of money. If I were to survey one hundred debt-laden couples and ask them whether more money would solve their financial problems, I can guarantee that over ninety percent would indicate that having more money would solve all of their financial problems. But I am also certain that a much different answer would be the result if the same question were posed to a group of one hundred financially astute couples that were not mired in a sea of debt. The difference in response would be attributable to financial literacy and also to discipline in the area of money management.

I strongly recommend financial counseling to couples that are constantly looking up from the bottom of the financial pit that they have dug for themselves. The problems exist because most people would rather spend money on items that bring about immediate gratification rather than taking a strategic, long-term approach to financial investing. And effective personal financial management often requires the aid of expert advice, and this is one area in which few people care to invest.

People who place a low premium on identifying the root causes of their current bad situations are doomed to remain in them. These individuals are the ones who always seem to take the road <u>most</u> traveled. Why continue on a path that continues to yield undesirable returns? People remain in financially discouraging situations because they lack the will and oftentimes the knowledge to disrupt the status quo they have allowed to accumulate around them, not because they want to. In most instances, a financial Boot Camp is in order.

Is there any hope for the many marriages besieged by overwhelming debt? Is it possible to reverse situations plagued by severe financial turmoil? An emphatic yes to both questions! Even a family with an occasional financial skirmish should take steps to get its financial house in order.

1. Who should handle the family's financial matters, husband or wife? Or should the one who makes the most money manage all financial concerns, simply by default?

Before I answer this question allow me to ask the following question. "Is it documented anywhere, in a marriage handbook or in the Bible, where the husband has ever been dubbed with this responsibility?" I think not. Nor does there exist any documented proof that the title of financial money manager has ever been conferred onto the wife. Who then should be responsible for the finances? The answer is quite simple. Whoever can perform the responsibility best should be the one to manage the family finances. Couples must seriously think long and hard about bringing in outside reinforcement (i.e. a bookkeeper) when neither of the two has the ability to accurately account for the income and expenses, if coming together still proves ineffective. Sharing the responsibility can, however, prove to be fun and a way of drawing the husband and wife closer together. The synergy of husband and wife coming together to develop a financial game plan will oftentimes prove to be more effective than one created by any of the partners alone.

2. What should we do if we can't see eye-to-eye on how the money should be spent?

If you are arguing over money matters, chances are there exist deeper issues that come into play in the relationship. In this case, money is only the scapegoat for your disharmony. In all instances, the art of skilled diplomacy and constant communication are always a must because both parties have a vested interest in the family's financial stability. I strongly encourage married individuals to keep each other informed of every transaction that will impact the family finances, despite whether one or both spouses work. Understand that the income producer's input does not outweigh that of the other individual who may be a stay at home spouse (usually the wife) or a full-time student. Also, the size of one's paycheck should never give one spouse a tie-breaking vote when it comes to decision-making. The key to survival on this front is constant communication.

3. What if one of the spouses has bad spending habits that lead to overextended charge accounts and bounced checks?

Returned checks and maxing out the credit cards are anathema to good money management. Constant use of credit will always trigger the payment of high interest rates while having your checks bounce their way back home will keep you paying exorbitant finance charges and fees. Let's suppose you have three bounced checks a month with a per check fee of thirty dollars. That totals ninety dollars a month. Then add an additional charge of thirty dollars per check for each company to which you wrote checks. You are now up to one hundred and eighty dollars, which gets subtracted from your account before any bills are paid. What remains is your net disposable income. In most family situations, people walk away each month with barely enough to satisfy their basic monthly obligations. This is a prescription for disaster because couples in this type of condition are always living on the brink of disaster. Never is there enough money to respond to emergencies or to enjoy some stress-relieving activities like taking a family vacation. Marriage becomes the first battlefield casualty under these conditions. It is a serious problem.

Regaining control of your family's finances must become your primary concern. Today's community property laws heavily penalize the uninformed. And failure to maintain good credit can make life very difficult when the need to purchase a home or car arises. For that reason, couples must fight hard to maintain excellent credit if they currently have it and work diligently to get it if they don't. Paying bills late reduces your credit worthiness and causes individuals with questionable payment histories to pay very high interest rates to secure loans.

Remember! The road to financial recovery begins with the recognition that you need help. And needing help is not shameful, but needing it and never reaching for it is. What you fail to take care of today will affect your children tomorrow. The longer you delay in turning your financial situation around, the more you withdraw from their tomorrows. With the plethora of possibilities available today to obtain capable assistance, you no longer need to cry foul; simply cry for help.

I strongly recommend my book, ***Building Wealth From The Ground Up*** along with the ***Workout Material***. You can go to my website at www.BuildingUWealth.com and find other tools that will help you improve your financial position.

Jotting Down Things to Remember

Jotting Down Things to Remember

Jotting Down Things to Remember

CHAPTER EIGHT

Houston, We Have A Communication Problem

*Good communication is a prerequisite to
experiencing a good marriage.*
-- Mikel Brown

CHAPTER EIGHT

Houston, We Have A Communication Problem

Humor: *A couple was asked, "What is your secret for staying married for such a long time?" "That's simple," one of them answered. "One of us talks and the other one doesn't listen!"*

I once surveyed a group of couples to see what they thought about what this joke suggested. I also asked them to tell me who they thought, husband or wife, was the one who "talks" and who was the one who "doesn't listen". I was amazed to discover an interesting fact concerning the perception of general communication between married couples. By asking couples which one of the two does the most talking and which one refuses to listen, I was able to make some strong conclusions regarding the dynamics of communication between husbands and wives. I realize, however, that my survey did not cover a large enough or diverse enough survey group to generalize my findings to the rest of the population of married couples at large. Nevertheless, the questions posed to the group reveal, in my opinion, a startling fact. I was able to conclude that wives do most of the talking while husbands perform the majority of the non-active listening.

When husbands and wives read the aforementioned joke, they assumed the same thing regarding who talks and who does not listen. While I do believe that men and women are predisposed to communicate and listen differently, I feel also that society plays a big role in perpetuating our beliefs about whether women talk more than men. In television sitcoms and on the big screen, men are usually portrayed as babbling idiots, incapable of connecting with their women on any level. Women, on the other hand, are portrayed as being overbearing, talkative nags concerned only about their feelings and from whose presence the husbands are always trying to escape. This is not the total picture. I am not suggesting that these scenarios do not exist; I am only saying that this is not the overall dilemma of married couples, at least not in the United States.

> *A major problem is that couples have a tendency to read body language instead of listening to audible articulation.*

Good communication is a prerequisite to experiencing a good marriage. I identified ten married couples that I believed to have wonderful marriages, and I asked them to identify certain topics that they felt could improve their relationships if addressed. I separated the men and women into two groups based on gender. The hands-down, #1 listed topic was "communication." Based on this response, there appears to be a whole lot of finger pointing going on or clear admission that neither party knows how to communicate. Oftentimes, communication problems arise because of misperceptions between individuals. A major problem is that couples have a tendency to read body language instead of listening to audible articulation. Why is this considered a problem? The answer is simple, married individuals do not understand how often and to what extent their body language undermines their verbal communication. A wife usually knows when her husband is sexually turned on. She is accustomed not only to the penetrating stares, but also to the changes in the intonation and inflection of his voice. And if they're within close proximity, he may give unsolicited body rubs or even go as far as to travel all the way to the kitchen to prepare her favorite sandwich, if she asks- what tremendous sacrifice.

> *Body language should not be the focus of communicating; understanding audible articulation should be the main aim of both individuals.*

How does non-verbal communication factor into the equation when the need for reassurance and intimacy are in competition for a spouse's preoccupation with other important matters? Non-verbal cues should not be the prime ingredients in communication between husbands and wives, but unfortunately they are. For example, a wife may conclude that her husband no longer finds her sexually appealing, when, in fact, his thoughts are consumed by the pressing thoughts of a pending business failure. If when talking to her husband she reads his reticence and occasional "Um hums" as apathy, assumptions will cause her mind to travel in the wrong direction entirely. By simply knowing where he is in terms of dealing with other issues, she would understand that lack of sexual attraction on his part is not the issue. Better communication on both parts could serve to allay her concerns and make her a better ally in his plight. The fault is not hers entirely, for he has an obligation to the preservation of the relationship to keep her plugged into his world, since it affects hers tremendously.

Body language should not be the focus of communicating; understanding audible articulation should be the main aim of both individuals. Unfortunately, it takes destroying old communication habits in order to start fresh, new ones. Some individuals believe that if they speak with a certain tone they will get better responses from their spouses. One couple, in particular, informed me that the raising of the voice seemed to be the only way of getting the other person's attention. I told them that this was a false conclusion that they had come to believe to be true. And in actuality, the raising of the voice was an unhealthy practice that they had woven into their verbal communications with each other, I went on to add. In other words, they developed a bad way of communicating with one another, and they had begun to accept it as standard practice.

> *Serious problems creep into the relationship when partners continue to misread the body language of their partners.*

Couples are very good at suggesting much more in their communication by making subtle use of tone variation, facial expressions, and voice inflections. Over time, partners in marital relationships develop an argot of their own that keeps others in the dark regarding what they are communicating. For example, couples can spot each other way across the room at a social gathering and give clear indication to each other that it's time leave without a single word ever being exchanged. The eyes and body language communicated the entire message.

One day I asked my wife how she knew that I wanted to leave this particular social gathering; her reply was, "I don't know. But you looked like you were ready to leave." She was absolutely correct. I communicated to her without ever opening my mouth or hinting with any verbal expression that I was ready to leave. Although most couples are masters at properly reading their partners' cues in instances like this, they fail to be adept at the same when it comes to their more private conversations.

A person can say the same thing as his or her spouse but in a different way.

Serious problems creep into the relationship when partners continue to misread the body language of their partners. Learning how to communicate effectively without distorting one's intentions is an art form that requires practice and takes a great deal of effort. By virtue of the fact that you are reading this book, I am certain that effective communication between you and your spouse is important to you. Therefore, work hard to improve the lines of effective dialogue with your spouse. Doing so signals, in no uncertain terms, to your partner that you are willing to be patient and do whatever it takes in order to accurately receive whatever it is he or she has to say.

Different upbringings dictate that two people will invariably communicate differently. And while you and your spouse may have enjoyed similar life experiences before coming together, you will now need to synchronize those experiences so that harmony can exist between you. The fact that husband and wife can say the same thing in different ways contributes to much of a couple's communication problems. Frustration results when two sane people struggle to be, not just heard, but understood.

Whenever I speak publicly, I carefully learn as much as I can about my audience so that I adjust my delivery to fit the audience. And even though I may deliver the same message to different audiences, I am mindful of the fact that even groups will process what I say differently. The odds of my being understood increases exponentially each time I tailor my message specifically to the audience addressed. Because words can have different meanings to different people, I iterate my points similar to if I was speaking from a thesaurus book.

Likewise, partners in marriage relationships must approach communication from the standpoint that what they think they are saying, chances are, is not what the other person is receiving. A person can say the same thing as his or her spouse but in a different way. Therefore, husbands and wives must be ever mindful to filter out any extraneous non-verbal cues that can undermine their intentions, and also they must carefully weigh the words used to ensure that what is intended is actually what gets communicated. Study your spouse carefully when he or she speaks so that your communication will get better as you grow together. If you do, you will never have to say, "Houston, we have a communication problem."

Jotting Down Things to Remember

Jotting Down Things to Remember

Jotting Down Things to Remember

CHAPTER NINE

For Couples Who Can't Find The Time

*If your priorities are out of order,
so will it be with how you spend your time.*
-- Mikel Brown

CHAPTER NINE

For Couples Who Can't Find The Time

We live in a fast paced society, which places great demands on people's time and energy. There are so many external factors pulling and competing for our time that it is very difficult to decide where our attention should be focused every waken minute. People have careers to build, college classes to attend, shopping to do, church to attend, homes to care for, children to nurture, personal financial portfolios to manage, spouses to spend time with, food to prepare, and finally time for "just me." Does it sound like too much to pack into one day? We live in the most active and demanding era in the history of mankind. Time is man's most precious commodity, and yet we give little consideration as to how best to spend it. If your priorities are out of order, so will it be with how you spend your time.

I have learned the hard way that God is not going to accommodate me by placing several more hours in a day just to enable me to accomplish what I could not perform in 24 hours. Every human on the planet gets only twenty-four hours every day to accomplish that day's tasks. Effective

For Couples Who Can't Find Time

time management is a skill that people must learn. It takes diligence to be a good steward of time. Failure to fulfill today's obligations means that more are added to tomorrow's. What you cannot get done today will have to wait until tomorrow. Therefore, we must be wise in how we use our time so that today's important issues get our attention before we start allocating precious attention to those of tomorrow. Most people are unskilled when it comes to prioritizing their daily agendas. Generally, it boils down to learning to say no to certain activities and people of less importance to your daily mission. It is not to say that people are not important; it's that every person's deadline and needs are not your responsibility to solve. And in many cases, not even your own grown children's agendas should keep you from fulfilling your own because they are responsible for making their own decisions in life.

Procrastination is the greatest thief of time.

Procrastination is the greatest thief of time. People who are often late to work are usually distracted by the programs on their televisions in the morning. An overwhelming number of people listed, on a questionnaire, watching television as the primary reason for their lateness to work, despite getting up on time. Have you ever looked at a television program while on your way out of the house, hoping to catch the end of a particular episode or the outcome of a sports game? Yes! Most of us are guilty of allowing the TV to rob us of precious seconds and minutes of every day. I am convinced that it is not the lack of time that people have problems with; it is the misappropriation of time that exposes our lack of discipline.

Focused, quality time with your family is far better than distracted, quantity time. What child or spouse wants to spend time with a person who, while with their family, is mentally preoccupied with a things-to-do-list? Spending time with your spouse and family is not work; it's your obligation.

> *Focused, quality time with your family is far better than distracted, quantity time.*

Some time ago, I spoke with a rather schedule-driven salesman who appeared to be overwhelmed by his schedules and deadlines. As we began to talk, his mobile phone rang. Politely excusing himself, he answered it. As he talked with the person on the other end, I could see that he was becoming very upset in his refusals to meet the other person at a particular time and place. He went on about what he could and could not do. I was under the impression that he was talking with a client. After he had hung up his phone, he apologized for the interrupting call from his wife. I couldn't help but laugh to myself because of how they were discussing scheduling their time together. I began imagining just how difficult it must be for the two of them to try and schedule every activity around his life and career.

I am saddened when I hear of situations where the children have taken a back seat to the careers of their parents. I can assure you that most wives are more content with trying to make the best of their marriages rather than sitting home alone because their husbands are chasing bigger and bigger paychecks. Nothing can replace the love of a parent or spouse. Work-a-holism is a poor substitute for love.

Let's try to figure out how two busy people can use their time efficiently and wisely. Sometimes couples try to spend time with their children when they should focus on spending time with one another. I am not all diminishing the importance of family time. I am simply pointing out that

> *Balance is the key to knowing where and how to spend valuable time with your spouse.*

couples should spend time together (sans children) that is used strictly for marital preventive maintenance. Balance is the key to knowing where and how to spend valuable time with your spouse. Do partners need to spend every day focusing on each other? Absolutely not! But they must be wise in how they make use of their available time together. They can take advantage of down time through the week, such as when the children have gone to bed early for school the next day. This time can be used for talking, cuddling, or simply watching television together. No extra money has to be spent on hotel accommodations or airline tickets. Time spent like this is a precursor to marital longevity.

50 Things To Do To Produce A Quality Marriage

Following is a list of 50 things you can do to begin the journey toward increasing quality time between you and your spouse. Remember that my focus here is only on married couples because marriage must always be in a constant state of repair in order to provide a healthy environment for the children.

How To Fix Your Marriage

1. Admit to being an undisciplined person.

2. If you are an undisciplined person by nature, ask God to give you the strength and determination to discipline your life and harness your time.

3. Go to your local bookstore and buy several books that will point out exercises you can do to develop discipline in your life.

4. Examine how your time is spent on a daily basis for two weeks, and from your observations, pinpoint the top ten areas where you spend the bulk of your time.

5. Two days after completing item 4 on this list, reexamine those top ten areas again to see if your priorities have changed.

6. Honestly admit to the areas of life you deem to be of the most importance to you.

7. Determine where your spouse ranks on your list of most importance.

8. Develop ways you can move your spouse higher on the list if they are not already.

9. Work on ways to reposition your job lower down the list, if it ranks ahead of your spouse and children.

10. Schedule times to simply surprise your spouse with something unexpected.

11. Learn how to work smarter on your job or

business, not longer.

12. Identify time spent unwisely, and convert it into quality time.

13. Don't be afraid to spend time alone with your spouse, without friends.

14. Attend church together on a regular basis.

15. Take in a movie at least once a month, sharing popcorn and soda.

16. Spend time together watching what your spouse enjoys watching on television.

17. Fight fatigue when you sit on the couch or lay in the bed together.

18. Drink hot beverages together during late evenings.

19. Avoid turning on the television every time you are in your bedroom together at night.

20. Practice speaking words of affection to your spouse.

21. Practice the kind of cuddling that doesn't necessarily lead to sex.

22. Hug and embrace each other passionately throughout the day.

23. Be loose and secretly pat your spouse on the butt

in public.

24. Learn to tease with one another without becoming offensive.

25. Dance with your spouse in your kitchen or living room in the presence of your children.

26. Call each other while at work just to say "I love you."

27. Occasionally take long lunches together before returning to work.

28. Don't take on other people's responsibilities at work so that you can leave at the appropriate time in order to spend time with your family.

29. Clean the house together.

30. Wash and fold clothes together.

31. Give time for your spouse to have some "Me time."

32. Walk in the mall together.

33. Window shop together without showing signs of restlessness.

34. Watch sports activities together, although you may not be interested.

35. Periodically visit friends and family members together.

36. Control your anger and never take anything out on your spouse.

37. Tell your spouse daily how much you love him or her.

38. When you have a disagreement, remember to talk about things other than what you disagreed over.

39. Always touch one another. Even find ways to rub up against one another when you're angry.

40. Don't be untouchable.

41. Lock arms often while you're walking together.

42. Talk about anything and everything, but never sit in a restaurant and be silent.

43. Have fun growing older together.

44. Never compare your marriage or experiences to that of another couple.

45. Never criticize your spouse for struggling with weight.

46. Make sure that you laugh, laugh and laugh together. (Laughter does well like medicine)

47. Wash the car together and later go cruising.

48. Stay young at heart.

49. Workout together.

50. Finally, keep God at the center of your marriage and family life. You are not the owner of your spouse, but a steward over your marriage. You will be held accountable for how you treated the gift God gave to you in the form of your spouse.

A person will become and grow to enjoy what they talk about and do all day long. If you would practice many of these points, you will never have to feel guilty about devoting time to a job because you will already have taken care of the most important things in the relationship. Your spouse will then know beyond a shadow of a doubt that your number one interest is to be with your family. This certainty is all the affirmation you need to foster a wonderful and loving relationship for the rest of your lives together.

Jotting Down Things to Remember

Jotting Down Things to Remember

CHAPTER TEN

For The Thrill Is Gone Marriage

How to Rekindle the Fire

*Love is not a fantasy;
it's a reality.*
*-- **Mikel Brown***

CHAPTER TEN

For The Thrill is Gone Marriage
How to Rekindle the Fire

Some years ago, B. B. King, the great blues guitarist and singer, had a top ten hit entitled, "The Thrill is Gone." The song was a depiction of a couple's relationship gone sour. The song did extremely well on record charts and at cash registers across the country. The success of this particular song was amazing, especially given the subject matter. I'm certain it did so well because many people were able to identify with the lyrics. Does the thrill leaving a marriage signal sure death to a once vibrant relationship? Is it true that once the thrill leaves a marriage it can never be regained? In most cases, couples allow the thrill to leave; once gone, they allow its absence to end the relationship. Don't be fooled by Hollywood's depictions of what marriage is because in the movie industry, fantasy masks reality and causes people to buy into fairy tale endings. Even the actors and actresses are caught up in this masquerade, as the astronomically high divorce rate among them proves. When the tape stops rolling and reality sets in, many actors and actresses are unable to deal with the realities of marriage. Hollywood is so unlike the real world, people should never look to the big screen for an example of how relationships should actually be. Sadly, however, many people do.

> **Perception, not appearance, is the key to attraction.**

When you truly love your spouse, the thrill can never truly diminish or disappear. It only gets buried beneath the debris of hurt, abuse, confusion, rejection or just plain everyday living. I have counseled many couples that have experienced times when they thought the thrill of romance was truly gone, only to discover that it had been displaced underneath the pain and disappointment caused by their spouse. Through effective counseling intervention, most couples are able to rediscover romance that had simply gone dormant. If the relationship is never pruned and nurtured, people tend to forget what drew them together in the first place. If this situation continues to persist, apathy will eventually give way to outright revulsion for the other person. But this does not have to be the result.

When the thrill seems to leave a relationship, a cold wind comes in to fill the void. In this situation, marriage goes from being a refuge of comfort to an arrangement of convenient cohabitation. Individuals begin walking on eggshells to avoid offending the other person. This becomes quite uncomfortable for all parties involved, even the children. When people fail to perform routine maintenance on their relationships, assumptions and other negative factors are permitted to fester between individuals. As a result, feelings are redirected from where they should go and are then consumed constantly on putting out scores of petty skirmishes. After a period of time, individuals become more focused on defending themselves rather than giving of themselves.

> *It's not what you say,*
> *but how you say it that counts.*

The excitement that once ruled your marriage can surface again once you discover how to combat the destructive forces that serve to undermine good relationships. Words are very powerful. You cannot continue to fire-off hurtful words at your spouse and expect that person to feel good about you. Words are like daggers, but they are more pernicious than knives because they have the ability to cut and rip apart one's very soul. It is impossible to undo the damage caused by destructive words when wounds are deep and left exposed to the elements of bad relationships for far too long. When the contaminants of hurting words set in, a more powerful healing agent must be applied to bring about, not just healing of the soul, but spiritual restoration. When pain gets to this point, only God has the power to restore the wounded heart. For this very reason, spouses must be very careful of the language used between each other. Remember! It's not what you say, but how you say it that counts.

Having been in the field of counseling as long as I have, I am often asked whether it is possible to love your spouse and not be sexually attracted to them. To this question, I answer with a resounding yes! Perception is the key to attraction. The truth is that outward appearance is of great importance when it comes to establishing one's attraction to another. Perception gives us the ability to see beyond skin-deep beauty to what truly lies beneath.

For The Thrill Is Gone Marriage

I once counseled a couple that had it all together, as far as outward packaging is concerned. She was a beautiful blond who was very articulate and extremely intelligent. Her husband was the picture of masculinity; he strutted finely chiseled muscles and an acute intellect. Yet, something was missing. He would often complain that she needed to work out more with him at the gym. He commented to her all the time about how she could stand to lose a pound or two, tighten up her thighs, stomach, and gluts, and work on firming her arms by lifting more weights. Looking at this woman made me feel as though I needed my eyes examined. Perhaps, I didn't look closely enough to see the flaws her husband saw. If she had ever asked me if I saw anything wrong with her appearance, I would have weighed in with an emphatic no because to me she was very attractive. Unfortunately, her husband paid no attention at all to her inner beauty, and she was full of that as well. Her husband lacked the ability to perceive her inner beauty, and as a result, he was brutally judgmental about her exterior. Needless to say, this relationship was constantly strained. It is very difficult for a marriage to survive under the constant weight of this kind of scrutiny and desire for perfection.

Sexual excitement is based on thought not on feelings.

Permit me to expose two major flaws that led to this man's distorted view of his wife. The first problem is found in what Shakespeare once said, *"The eye sees not itself."* If you think that you are already perfect, you will have no tolerance or respect for those who are not. It is easy to judge yourself by the weaknesses of others, and judge others by your strengths. It is human nature to be more lenient with ourselves than we are with others. The husband simply focused on those things about his wife that he did not like about himself. He is guilty of what psychiatrist call "projecting." This reminds me of a situation that happened to my wife a few years ago. A woman once gave my wife a pie as a kind gesture, hoping it would lead to friendship. She said to my wife, "I know that you don't like me, so I made you a pie." My wife hardly knew the lady, and certainly not enough to dislike her. This woman was actually trying to project onto my wife secret feelings she had harbored about my wife all along.

The second problem this husband had was the "perfect body" image he had fixed in his mind against which he would compare his wife. Perception is based on prior information, and prior information can warp the present views we have of others. It did in his case. For example, men who frequently masturbate tend to have difficulty relating to their spouses sexually. These individuals tend to enjoy fantasizing about women in magazines more than engaging in actual sexual intercourse with their spouses. Sex itself becomes a secondary means to gratification- second to the stimulation of masturbation.

In many of my counseling sessions, couples have discussed their disappointments in the bedroom. Masturbation after sexual intercourse was discovered to occur with at least seventy percent of the couples counseled. Most often, women share that they prefer for their partners to gently touch and caress them, whereas ninety percent of men reveal that they are more turned on by thoughts of an imaginary sex partner. This led me to conclude that men, in general, search for sexual satisfaction from their imaginations rather than from their emotions. With most men, sexual arousal is triggered more by thoughts than by feelings.

For The Thrill Is Gone Marriage

Can you ever recall watching a movie or some particular television show that caused you to get angry, become sad, laugh, or even cry? What was it that evoked your emotions? It was the words you heard. Words create thoughts; thoughts create pictures; and pictures stimulate your emotions. When couples say that the thrill is gone from their relationships, they are usually referring to absence of those beautiful words that used to create so many wonderful and exiting emotions during the courtship phase. Now that those words are exchanged less in marriage, individuals mistakenly conclude that love no longer exists.

When love truly consumes an individual, superficial things just don't matter. Additional weight added over the years, thinning or complete hair loss, and even removal of a breast due to cancer are all of little consequence when true love dominates a relationship. It is possible to find your spouse just as romantically appealing after 20+ years of marriage as the day you married them, even after Father Time has done his handy work. Sincere love provides people with a perspective that tends to highlight inner beauty and downplay those superficial external qualities. The more I age, the more I thank God for giving my lovely wife glasses with this special power.

But the moment individuals begin to compare their spouses against images in magazines, unrealistic perceptions begin to paint their partners in a negative light. All of a sudden, wives wish that they could be swept off their feet by Brad Pitt, while men start to fantasize about waking up next to Halle Berry. Before you know it, spouses begin to take each other for granted, or they may even put undo pressure on the other person to make drastic changes. There is nothing wrong with you wanting your spouse to lose weight in order to become healthier and more active. But something is seriously wrong when your reason for wanting your spouse to lose weight is to avoid the embarrassment of being seen together in public with someone you are ashamed of.

If the sparks seems to have dissipated from your marriage, check the images you have allowed into your mind. The sparks can indeed return, but it can't as long as poor images cause you to disregard the value of the precious person to whom you are connected. So, get rid of all the pornography if you have it; it's only hurting your cause. And there is no need to bring in the cavalry to add spice; you and your partner are enough. Many of the tactics that couples employ to add spice to their relationships are the very things that destroy them. The answer is not found in gadgets and stand-ins; healthy change in your marriage will be discovered when you change the perception you have of your spouse.

Set aside one day to simply take stock of the feelings you have concerning your spouse. Reflect on the times when the two of you would just sit and talk for hours about nothing, simply enjoying each other's presence. I'm certain you can recall those precious times if you try hard enough. "What's my motivation?" you ask. You have invested years of precious tears, love and energy into something you once esteemed as precious as life itself. For did you not vow to remain together until death would separate the two of you? You pledged a lifetime of commitment to your spouse, or were your words vain and void of meaning. Look beyond your current predicament to the possibilities of tomorrow. Don't focus at this moment on all the problems you have been through together. Don't even consider the slight imperfections that exist in your spouse, such as balding, excess weight, or stretch marks from childbirth- imperfections that did not exist when you exchanged vows.

Understand that beneath these superficial flaws, the same person still resides on the inside of that house, which is the body. While the body has undergone many changes, the person you used to be so in love with remains the same. When you go through this exercise, you'll discover that you have much for which to be thankful. Additionally, your perception of your spouse will begin to take a new shape.

Next, practice the little things you loved doing while you were dating. Call each other during the day just to say hello. Show that you care by asking how his or her day is going. The small things we do for our spouses oftentimes carry more weight than many of the big gestures because they reveal a concern and thoughtfulness that is genuine. Taking someone out to dinner is fine; making that person's favorite meal is far better. Do not use this occasion to discuss serious matters like finances, bills, or problems with the children. Those issues can wait for another time. Right now you two are the most important people in each other's lives.

Many couples forget how to focus on their marriage after children enter the picture. Never regard your children as an interruption, but see them as part of the healthy, family environment that the two of you have built together. Children need to see the loving affection their parents have for one another so that they will grow up with a healthy and wholesome image of marriage. Everything that I have shared with you in this chapter will help to restore the thrill of your marriage. If you adhere to what I have outlined herein, you will discover where you last buried the thrill of the relationship. Once you apply these principles, you will no longer desire the fantasy world of Hollywood because you will desire the love of your own wife or husband.

Learn to celebrate yourself and your spouse. Nothing in

your marital relationship will change on its own. Therefore, it will take committed effort. For some, it will take a lot of work to produce the type of change desired. In the end, however, you'll find that any effort expended was worth the investment. True love gives all and doesn't hold back. Persist in this until you can honestly say, "The thrill is back!"

Jotting Down Things to Remember

Jotting Down Things to Remember

CHAPTER ELEVEN

Pillow Talk

How to Turn Your Bedroom into Your Playground

The secret to experiencing an exciting, healthy and wholesome sexual relationship between a husband and wife is to keep it a secret.
-- Mikel Brown

CHAPTER ELEVEN

Pillow Talk

How to Turn Your Bedroom into Your Playground

Before I go any further into this subject, let's get a few things straight. First, what a married couple does in the privacy of their own home is their business. A couple's private dalliances should be guarded and kept in secret compartments in their hearts, never to be discussed among friends and or relatives. Secondly, sex or love making, whatever you want to call it, should never be regarded as taboo or forbidden subject matter between a husband and wife. Very few couples, especially Christian couples, ever seriously broach this topic. This is regretful because this is one of the most damaging areas of marriage. Sex is at the top of the list of leading contributing causes of divorce. As such, it should never be relegated to an area of little importance in the marital relationship. Thirdly, sex should never be looked upon as unholy, nasty, or as a necessary evil. Sex in a marriage relationship is holy and ordained by God Himself.

In truth, God created sex for the purpose of procreation and pleasure. From the act of sex, children are added to the planet, for the glory of God. And for their services, God equipped husband and wife to pleasure one another in the process. Over the years, however, this God-ordained act has become twisted and distorted in the minds of many people. Pornography, X/R-rated movies, Hollywood, and even regular TV have done a lot to promote the unhealthy image that most people have regarding sexual intercourse. As a result, it remains one of those activities in which people love to participate but never want to discuss openly. Contaminated views of sex have led to a great deal of bedroom dysfunction.

I have often had to work with couples to help them get over the pain of infidelity. Infidelity adversely impacts a marriage in two ways. In the first instance, the innocent person is devastated by the breech of covenant. And in the second instance, the hurting spouse is then unable to freely give his or her body to the person who cheated. The inability to get over the mental thoughts of a spouse's cheating is not something that can go away by the waving of a wand. It is those plaguing thoughts that shut down one partner's willingness to surrender sexually to the other. In this case, there is no easy answer to unlocking the gift inside the hurting individual. Many people believe that affairs destroy relationships, but in reality, it is a small part of the reason. The problem after an affair is the victim's struggle to deal with the pain and anguish.

If you secretly compare, you will openly compete.

One of the things I tell people to do after experiencing such an ordeal is to never secretly compare yourself to the person with whom your spouse had an affair. Do not allow your imagination to wander or ask questions regarding what was done and how it was done. That is of no consequence to you. If you secretly compare, you will openly compete. How do you compete with images? The truth of the matter is that you can never compete with your manufactured images of another's performance; you will always leave the mental episode more hurt and upset. So, fight to let go of what is not important to your well being.

If you are the one who's been hurt, and have voiced your thoughts to forgive and continue working on your marriage, open up communication lines with your spouse and let him or her know your inhibitions. Ask your spouse to be patient and to help you through this painful period. If your spouse asks how she or he can be there for you, please do not say "give me space". Space between married couples can be more damaging and devastating to your efforts when it comes to strengthening what remains of an already fragile relationship. Just say you don't know, but when you figure things out, you'll let them know. In the meantime, allow your spouse to embrace you and your pain so that the process of healing can begin. Don't allow your mind to run wild with thoughts that your spouse is getting away with their infidelity without any negative repercussions. Understand that they too are suffering from the guilt of knowing that they've caused you tremendous pain. For more on this topic, refer to the chapter *Successfully Overcoming the Pain of an Affair*.

The lack of knowledge and information is usually what prevents most couples from enjoying the kind of intercourse that is mutually gratifying.

Pillow Talk

If you are like most couples, you may be experiencing a bit of a struggle in the bedroom. This is not to suggest that your marriage isn't good, it simply reveals that sex with your spouse is not one of the high points of your marriage. Perhaps you've never had great sex with your spouse; although, you long to experience wild nights of passionate love making with your spouse. The lack of knowledge and information is usually what prevents most couples from enjoying the kind of intercourse that is mutually gratifying. Acquiring the proper information will help you to release your inhibitions and provide you with the necessary communication skills to better relate your desires to your spouse.

Most couples start off their marriages with fantastic, trophy-winning sex. But after the wife has had one or more children, things begin to change rather quickly. Not only does her body go through tremendous physical changes, but her mindset regarding intercourse is altered as well. As God intended, the nurturing of newly arriving children becomes the focus of her energy, leaving the husband to reminisce about how sex use to be before the children came along. At this point, most husbands are desperately trying to figure out what went wrong or if she has lost her sexual desire for him. Sex becomes a quick flurry of "Hurry, before the children wake up", after which the partners retreat back to their parental routines. Make no mistake about it, sex changes after several years of marriage and children. But it also can get better if both spouses are willing to admit their desires and submit to surrendering to the wishes of the other.

Dr. Brown, "Are you suggesting that I perform some of those wild antics my spouse has been just storing away in that fantasy-filled mind." Yes, within reasonable boundaries. I am not suggesting that you try to mimic the lascivious acts of some X-rated porn star. Nor am I suggesting that everything portrayed in X-rated movies is off limits either. The Bible states that the marriage is honorable in all and the bed is undefiled. In other words, what is done behind closed doors between a husband and wife, with the exception of anal penetration, is considered private and within the context of the Scriptures. What should be clearly understood by both partners is that each is to service the sexual needs of the other partner, without condemnation.

One woman was interested in telling me the problems that she and her husband were having in the bedroom. I asked her not to go into detail about her husband's apparent problem without him being present. "Have you discussed any of your concerns with your spouse?" I asked. Her reply was, "He simply wouldn't understand." The problem was not difficult to solve, it was simply a matter of matching desire with schedule. They both seemed to enjoy each other in the bedroom, but she simply desired to have sex more often than he did. She would often feel rejected when he failed to pick up on the signals. I discovered that their problem wasn't only the result of sexual infrequency, but it was also due to a misunderstanding of what she considered lady-like behavior. You see, her mother always told her that it is not lady-like to approach your husband for intercourse. So, she would wait for him to approach her. On the other hand, he believed that sex should occur on an equal opportunity basis. He felt that his wife should approach sometimes and that he shouldn't be the only one in the relationship making the advancements. Several years went by with them holding their thoughts captive instead of releasing them. If they had addressed this problem earlier, they would have avoided many years of mental anguish and sexual frustration. They later expressed how just a little information heeded brought a lot of joy into the bedroom.

Pillow Talk

Romantic love is deeply embedded in American culture and has been for more than a century and a half. Its effect upon contemporary life is not to be underestimated. In our

> ***In our culture, to be married and not experience romantic love constitutes true deprivation.***

culture, to be married and not experience romantic love constitutes true deprivation. From childhood we have been conditioned to believe that romance and love are synonymous. We are consumed with the need to experience romance at all cost. Ridiculous <u>un</u>reality TV shows such as The Bachelor, The Bachelorette, and Want To Marry A Millionaire serve only to heighten this desire. It seems that people are fanatical about experiencing romance, whether actual or vicariously on TV or the big screen. Television and Hollywood have both done a great injustice to our children by portraying sex as the ultimate fulfillment of love. Moreover, television has used sex to sell everything from tooth paste to cars. With these images constantly coming across our television screens, it makes it difficult for young people especially to differentiate between what is real and what is fantasy.

Most people have distorted concepts of love and romance. Sad to say, but many Christians make sex out to be a non-pleasurable experience. Most couples' bedroom problems stem from an inability to completely relax and release themselves to their partners. Holding back one's love and affection is one of the worst things an individual can do to the person they love. It is not a sin to enjoy your mate on an intimate and physical level. And yes, you can even talk about what pleases you and what doesn't. If you can't talk to your spouse about such intimate matters, to whom do you turn for answers to your concerns?

For People Who Struggle with Sexual Gratification

Allow me to answer a few questions that have consistently been raised during my many years of counseling. I will appropriately call these questions FYI.

▶ Is it right to experience sexual enjoyment and pleasure?

Many couples suffer in the bedroom because of their distorted view of what is permissible and what isn't. The Bible mentions how marriage is honorable in all and the bed is undefiled. This means that your bedroom activity is your business. In addition to this, sex is not a necessary evil but a time of pleasure and enjoyment between two people who love each other. Sexual intercourse was designed by the Creator Himself; therefore, it is completely right for married people to enjoy sex for not only procreation but also for recreation, as well.

▶ Is everything authorized with my spouse?

Absolutely! God called the marriage bed undefiled. Sex is more than intercourse; it is the highest form of intimacy between a husband and wife. And it should never be viewed as degrading and disgraceful. In fact, the marriage bed refers to sexual intercourse and all activity leading up to it.

▶ How often should a couple have intercourse?

What God deems as the right frequency is left to the creators of those moments- meaning you and your spouse. Some sex therapists suggest a minimal of twice a week. I strongly disagree with regulated sexual intercourse. Sexual habits and needs vary from one person to the next and therefore it is difficult to suggest a general rule of thumb. Newlyweds usually engage in intercourse three to five times a week and sometimes even twice a day. Many of them subconsciously feel as though they are catching up for loss time. Young married men act as though sex is trying to get away from them or as though they can fill up on it. Let me give it to you in a nutshell. Intercourse should occur as often as needs arise in the relationship, giving consideration to any physical impairments or limitations. As couples get older and get bombarded with the issues of careers and child rearing, sexual appetites lessen.

▶ Is fantasizing about another person wrong?

Fantasizing is not a sin; it is a matter of what you fantasize about. People daydream about many things, but harnessing your thoughts is the key to a healthy and wholesome relationship. Allowing your imagination to run wild is dangerous for any married couple, even if the partners are seeking new ways to invigorate their sex lives. Thinking about another person is adultery in its rawest form. Jesus talked about how powerful our imagination is that He declared that if a man looked on a woman, after lust, he has already committed adultery in his heart. This kind of fantasizing will lead to unfaithfulness and ultimately to divorce.

▶ Can masturbation ever be appropriate?

Masturbation is a serious problem among individuals

and married couples. Many people have not learned how to cope with the body's desire for sexual fulfillment. Consequently, people who don't understand the power of their imaginations tend to lack the power of self-control. It is reported that better than 85% of all males confess to masturbating at some time during their life. The percentage of women who confess to masturbating is slightly lower than that of men. Many single people, including Christians, see no harm in masturbation because they feel that they are meeting a personal need without committing a sexual sin. The truth of the matter is that most people who engage in masturbation end up taking this practice into their marriages. The main reason people continue to masturbate after getting married is that their actual intercourse does not live up to the standard of their fantasies while masturbating. How can a spouse compete with a mental image that can produce as real a gratifying experience as the physical act itself? Many people who masturbated frequently during their youth and early adulthood have confessed that after having sex with their partners, they had difficulty fighting off the urge to masturbate. As with anything in life, what substitutes as the real makes unnecessary the actual. Therefore, masturbation tells your spouse that their services are not necessary. How hurting this realization must be.

Is there any time that masturbation can be within the confines of what is permissible? Yes, there are situations that are allowable. A couple can engage in the masturbation of one another during foreplay. The Bible doesn't say that touching the genital of your spouse is wrong. In fact, it is honorable. I will address more about touching the genitals of your spouse in the next question.

▶ Is Oral Sex wrong?

Pillow Talk

I have discovered that people have many sex related questions that they would simply like to hear answered from someone other than a sex therapist on television who doesn't reflect their convictions. Some of the questions stem from the fact that many people have morals they wish not to violate. With the sexual permissiveness and its pervasiveness in our society, people feel freer to discuss this sensitive subject. On the other hand, Christians do not feel as free to come out of the closet to discuss this and other important sexual issues. As a result of this false modesty, many Christian couples are confused and have a greater propensity to engage in pornography.

Let's get a quick understanding of what oral sex actual is. Oral sex is the stimulation of the sexual organs by using one's mouth and tongue. You will find as many theologians lining up on one side of this issue as you will find on the other side. Since there are many Bible teachers who disagree over the issue of oral sex, I want to be extremely careful and sensitive as to how I address this particular topic. Allow me to make the following disclaimer: By my comments stated herein, I neither avow nor disavow my personal position on this matter. I suggest that you refrain from engaging in oral sex if it goes against your deeply held beliefs. This subject should be discussed thoroughly and openly between a husband and wife in cases where one spouse wants it and the other wants nothing to do with oral sex.

No spouse should demand oral sex from his or her spouse. The aim of sexual gratification is to please your spouse, not yourself. If your spouse doesn't feel comfortable with oral sex, you should never condemn them or conclude that they do not love you. Remember there is more than one way to skin a cat. Be considerate and loving. Your spouse will respond to your sensitivity by giving you all the loving you need. Over time the person's views may change in this area as they realize that you are more concerned with their well-being than with your own. If you hold oral sex as one of the expressions of love, with subtle concern, voice it and assure your spouse that you will not press the issue and when they are ready to discuss it, you will be patient and understanding.

► Can we watch an X-rated film to help us with our love life?

This is similar to desiring that others can join in your sexual experience. Dismantle the walls you have constructed around you that prevents you from communicating your desires to your spouse. Why watch pornography when you will only end up polluting your mind with toxic thoughts and vain images of someone's concept of how you should perform in the bedroom. Do you really want to measure yourself against carefully scripted and rehearsed pornographic scenarios? Instead, discover the pleasure that sexual improvisation with your spouse can bring. Use your own imagination to find new and exiting ways for the two of you to satisfy one another.

When it comes to the bedroom, you and your spouse set the rules. God has given the two of you a blank check to fill out however you so choose when it comes to satisfying your own spouse. Be aware, however, of His few stipulations. Remember, the goal of sexual pleasure is that you work to satisfy your partner's needs. If that is the aim of you both, who is then shortchanged in the process?

Jotting Down Things to Remember

Jotting Down Things to Remember

CHAPTER TWELVE

Understanding How To Love Your Spouse

Everything we do in life requires discipline.
-- Mikel Brown

CHAPTER TWELVE

Understanding How To Love Your Spouse

Humor: *When a certain man was informed of a marriage seminar, he said, "The marriage seminar is a good idea. I'm going to send my wife so that she can tell me how it helped her."*

> "I think you can be madly in love with someone you would be sick of after ten weeks; and I'm pretty sure you can be bound heart and soul to someone about whom you don't at that moment feel excited, any more than you feel about yourself." --*C. S. Lewis*

My aim in this particular chapter is to give you an abridged overview of a few principles that will help govern and guide a marriage to success. My goal is not to induce information overload by inundating you with voluminous commentary on how to love your spouse. I am confident that a small dose of truth will suffice. It will serve as the point of departure as you begin to understand your role in marriage. Your human effort will prove to be the major contribution to the success of your relationship with your spouse. My friend, please do not underestimate the tremendous selfless sacrifices and labor involved just to make a marriage work. When a couple succeeds in developing a good marital relationship, they have successfully learned how to embrace each other's differences and love one another without partiality.

Your marriage will succeed or fail based on the amount of accumulated information you have stored in your mental data bank. Simply having information safely tucked away in the mind is not enough; you must be willing to act on the information you have. Everything we do in life requires discipline. Discipline helps you to maintain control and keeps you from exceeding the boundaries or breaking the law. If we discipline ourselves in life, we are assured a certain amount of success.

Love is one of the greatest and most powerful forces given to mankind. It is also the most misunderstood emotion we have. Love exists within our hearts without any qualifiers to dictate what we should love. We are capable of loving things that are bad for us as much as we are able to love things from which we derive great benefit. Love does not discriminate. Additionally, everyone has the potential to love greatly and the capacity to receive abundant love. The biggest problem is that people do not fully understand what love truly is. Most married individuals have the wrong concept of love. Many people demand to be loved a certain way but are unwilling to give that same measure of love to another.

It is possible to be truly loved and not know it. If you cannot define what love is, it can come and go without you suspecting it. This then is truly a problem. For how can a person legitimately claim not be receiving love from his or her spouse when that individual has not gotten a handle on how to give pure love to the one from whom it is expected. In the course of loving, one soon learns that human relationships are not altogether sweet and simple, as it might first appear.

> *Romantic love alone lacks the resources to contend with conflicts successfully.*

The word I am looking for here is ambivalence, which means that within the same person there are opposing feelings. It is best illustrated in the quarrel involving two childhood friends who become angry with each other. Their parents reprimand them and tell their perspective child to come inside the house. The two friends were so angry at one another that they said, "I will never play with you again! I'll see you tomorrow."

If ambivalence is allowed to fester, divorce will soon take its place. There must reside on the inside of each spouse a burning ember to ignite hope for the relationship, in the darkest hours especially. The essence of true love is not revealed when all is well; it is manifested at times of great trials and testing. Although it was always there, love is suppose to step to the forefront of relationships and speak loudly on behalf of the two lovers whenever they together face the crucibles of life.

Individuals will experience the full range of emotions in every marriage relationship. Times of strong attraction will be counterbalanced by occasions of momentary disinterest.

Understanding How To Love Your Spouse

Desires for closeness will compete for times of disconnectedness. Passion will sometimes give way to indifference. There will come times when you like your spouse and times when you dislike the person, for whatever reason. True, mature love should be present to enable couples to deal with the different emotions that will blow through every relationship. Love is evidenced by emotion but confirmed by commitment and caring.

On the other hand, romantic love will never be able to stand under the constant weight of proving that all marriages will inevitably endure. When individuals come together as a result of romantic feelings alone, negatives will always outweigh positives, despite how few negatives there are as compared to the positives. Marriage was never meant to be based on romance. It is too fleeting a feeling to contain hope for tomorrow. Disenchantment will be the result with every relationship predicated on romance alone. Romantic love alone lacks the resources to contend with conflicts successfully.

Infatuation is as dissimilar from love as fantasy is from reality.

What is the difference between infatuation and love? This is a good question. Many people get married on the basis of having what they call great premarital sex. No real foundation exists in these instances, but there is tremendous fascination. Infatuation blinds people so that reality is masked from plain view. You may be under the spell of infatuation if you think your partner is as sexy as Brad Pitt, as talented as Denzel Washington, as noble as Ralph Nader, as funny as Rodney Dangerfield, and as athletic as Michael

Jordan. Love exists when you realize that he's as sexy as Rodney Dangerfield, as smart as Michael Jordan, as funny as Ralph Nader, as athletic as Denzel Washington, and looks nothing like Brad Pitt in any shape, form or fashion–but you desire him anyway. Infatuation is as dissimilar from love as fantasy is from reality. Although they share similar qualities, the two should never be confused. Doing so could mean trouble for a marriage.

How do I know if I'm under the spell of true love or romantic infatuation? If you don't know the answer to this question and you are already married, you may soon be headed to the divorce court. If you are contemplating marriage, I would advise you not to get married until you can answer this question truthfully. In marriage, romantic myths account for a great deal of disappointment and disillusionment. Married couples fall into the trap of trying to duplicate how things were during their days of courtship. Seldom, and I do mean seldom, will you ever find a married couple that has never experienced serious challenges to their love and communication. Trying to reproduce the past will create tremendous challenges in the future. It is natural to want things to be similar to the fanciful days of dating, but it is unrealistic to think that you can recreate those conditions inside your present marital relationship. First of all, married couples must contend with an entirely different set of responsibilities and commitments that dating couples do not, or should I say "should not". Secondly, nothing can compare to the whimsical, romantic feelings that engulf the hearts of individuals who are blinded by puppy love.

How to love your spouse is a question that has baffled every person, at one time or another, who has ever been in a committed relationship. Wives think that they have the answers to this question while husbands feel as though they hold the key to this mystery. In either case, neither are fully aware of how love should properly be expressed. Getting to the heart of this matter is both difficult and tiresome. Solving this enigma is like trying to put together a million-piece puzzle. Falling in love is easy; staying in love is laborious.

> *The rudiments of how to love each other should be discovered while spending valuable time together.*

So, how should I love you? Because everyone sees loves differently, answering this question is not easy to do. During courtship, individuals are too busy having fun and flirting with one another to truly get to the business of discovering one another's needs and desires. Courting isn't the same as marriage. In fact, the word courting has its root in the following meanings: (1) the art of flirting, (2) playful come-on, (3) seduction, (4) wink at, (5) connive, (5) plot, or (6) conspire. When this is the origin of a relationship, it will be expected throughout the entire marriage. A marriage cannot survive on child's play. It needs a much firmer foundation so that as the years go by, the marriage will not crack under the weight of normal wear and tear. The rudiments of how to love each other should be discovered while spending valuable time together.

If a man says poetically to his wife that "My love for you is like a ship on the ocean", he had better add, "And sometimes it gets so windy and stormy that he feels like jumping ship." Truly loving your spouse means that you are willing to accept that person's good and bad qualities. This is what makes love so unique. True love sees imperfection in an individual and still desires to be with that person.

A person who really understands true love realizes that love is always evident in how you see your mate, not by how you want to see them. You don't close your eyes to their

> *Wives demonstrate love for their husbands by respecting them.*

human flaws with the thought that you can later change the person. Your spouse's life experiences make that person who he or she is. Imperfection speaks to our humanity. Every person who has lived on planet earth, with the exception of Jesus Christ, has shortcomings that they are trying to overcome.

Wives demonstrate love for their husbands by respecting them. A wife's respect for her husband is the highest form of love she can possibly demonstrate, and it should second only to her love for Christ. The word "reverence", as stated in the Bible and when applied to marriage vows, suggests that she should perform the following: (1) respect and notice him, (2) regard him, (3) honor him, (4) prefer him, (5) venerate and esteem him, (6) yield to him, (7) praise him, and (8) love and admire him. If a

> *Love your wife like you love yourself; give your life for her and thus have no life remaining for yourself.*

wife doesn't believe that her husband should be respected in this manner, she must not expect to see herself as his queen. A man wants to come home to his castle because there she makes him feel like a king.

The way a husband is to demonstrate his love towards his wife is by crowning her queen of his castle. A husband is to esteem his wife as high as his own life. When a woman believes that she is genuinely loved, diamonds, fancy cars, and a big house will pale in comparison to her husband's love. Being and feeling loved becomes the apex of her existence. Despite the many hardships women have suffered at the hands of dishonest and calculating men, most every woman desires to lift up and praise the man who loves her unconditionally. When I think of my wonderful relationship with my wife, I can only conclude that I am blessed to have loved such a woman. I admonish every man to love your wife like you love yourself; give your life for her and thus have no life remaining for yourself. This is how I truly love my wife.

When wives truly respect their husbands as the Bible declares they should and when husbands are willing to die for their wives as Jesus says they must, then and only then will spouses truly understand how to love each other. When this occurs, all of your questions on this particular topic will have been answered within your heart.

Jotting Down Things to Remember

Jotting Down Things to Remember

Jotting Down Things to Remember

CHAPTER THIRTEEN

Redeemable Love Coupons

*Love should not be earned nor solicited,
but rather freely given and received.*
-- Mikel Brown

CHAPTER THIRTEEN

Redeemable Love Coupons

This chapter is more like a prudent admonishment to those who review this book. Every reader is encouraged to practice the marriage principles in this book on a continual basis. Do not be so quick to give up in your efforts to make your marriage better when things are not going according to plan. But continue working to improve yourself so that you can offer to your spouse the best you that you can be. If you are not yet married, please do not enter into the marriage covenant unadvisedly. Love is a wonderful thing, but it is difficult to detect its authenticity.

The redeemable Love Coupons offered in this chapter are not to be redeemed on an earned or merit basis. Your spouse should not have to feel as though they must work to earn special treatment from you of any kind, but that you should be willing to share the best of you. These coupons should be redeemed on selected days and it should be discretionary. Free days for redeeming your Love Coupons on weekdays should also be taken in consideration so that your weekends are not always scheduled but impromptu. These Love Coupons are designed to increase fun and excitement into your relationship; Ready, Get Set, Go!

Disclaimer: Redeem your Love Coupons at your own risk. Pregnancy has been known to occur unexpectedly.

Jot Down The Things That You Enjoyed When Using Your Love Coupons

✂ Cut Here

This love coupon redeemable for

Pillow fight!

(...followed by a little pillow talk!)

✂ Cut Here

This love coupon redeemable for

A $150 purchase

(...no questions asked.)

✂ Cut Here

This love coupon redeemable for

An Evening of Wild, Abandoned, Passionate _____!

✂ Cut Here

This love coupon redeemable for

Body Massage

(...with or WITHOUT our clothes)

✂ Cut Here

✂ Cut Here

Please Cut Out & Present To Your Spouse to Redeem

✂ Cut Here

Please Cut Out & Present To Your Spouse to Redeem

✂ Cut Here

Please Cut Out & Present To Your Spouse to Redeem

✂ Cut Here

Please Cut Out & Present To Your Spouse to Redeem

✂ Cut Here

✂ Cut Here

This love coupon is redeemable for

Uninterrupted conversation

...you listen ONLY

✂ Cut Here

This love coupon is redeemable for

Dinner - Just the 2 of US!

at my favorite restaurant... _____

✂ Cut Here

This love coupon is redeemable for

One BIG wet kiss

or two or three or ...

✂ Cut Here

This love coupon is redeemable for

Uninterrupted

Sporting Event Watching

...with the fellas and snacks!

✂ Cut Here

✂ Cut Here

Please Cut Out & Present To Your Spouse to Redeem

✂ Cut Here

Please Cut Out & Present To Your Spouse to Redeem

✂ Cut Here

Please Cut Out & Present To Your Spouse to Redeem

✂ Cut Here

Please Cut Out & Present To Your Spouse to Redeem

✂ Cut Here

✂ Cut Here

This love coupon is redeemable for

Romantic Evening

(...ALONE without the kids!)

✂ Cut Here

This love coupon is redeemable for

A Day of House Chores

(... yours and MINE!)

✂ Cut Here

This love coupon is redeemable for

You cook my favorite meal

...in a lingerie or briefs & you'll be my dessert!

✂ Cut Here

This love coupon is redeemable for

Get Out of the Dog House FREE CARD

(...ONE Night Only!)

✂ Cut Here

✂ Cut Here

Please Cut Out & Present To Your Spouse to Redeem

✂ Cut Here

Please Cut Out & Present To Your Spouse to Redeem

✂ Cut Here

Please Cut Out & Present To Your Spouse to Redeem

✂ Cut Here

Please Cut Out & Present To Your Spouse to Redeem

✂ Cut Here

✂ Cut Here

This love coupon is redeemable for

GIRLS Night Out

(...ONE Night Only!)

✂ Cut Here

This love coupon is redeemable for

One Evening of
NO TELEVISION
"just talk"

(...after the children are in bed)

✂ Cut Here

This love coupon is redeemable for

FELLAS' Night Out

(...ONE Night Only!)

✂ Cut Here

This love coupon is redeemable for

Full Control Over The
Remote Control

(...ONE Night Only!)

✂ Cut Here

✂ Cut Here
- -

Please Cut Out & Present To Your Spouse to Redeem

✂ Cut Here
- -

Please Cut Out & Present To Your Spouse to Redeem

✂ Cut Here
- -

Please Cut Out & Present To Your Spouse to Redeem

✂ Cut Here
- -

Please Cut Out & Present To Your Spouse to Redeem

✂ Cut Here
- -

"Quotes" for Marital Bliss

CHAPTER 1
Falling in love is easy;
staying in love is laborious.

Nations, whose families are fragmented,
have no continuity and their fabric is ripping at the seams....................3

A marriage is not held together simply because it is an institution;
it is held together because of its right content...6

Marriage is not a war; it is a love affair 7

CHAPTER 2
Expecting success without preparation is like
preparing without an agenda.

Companionship is valuable, but not critical...20

The secret pains of your potential spouse will eventually
become your public war, if you don't take steps to address them.......24

Investigate, but don't interrogate!..25

Financial illiteracy helps to form an unhealthy attitude about money.27

Trust is the foundation for a long, healthy relationship.......................28

Premarital abstinence may not be the popular thing to do,
but it will certainly prove to be the right thing....................................28

It is not until you are fully immersed in the commitment
of marriage that you can appreciate its benefits...................................30

An infatuation is an illusion of a self-manufactured assumption........33

CHAPTER 3
Children lack the maturity to fully weigh the consequences of
their actions. Therefore, if you desire a spouse,
find a responsible man or woman, not a boy or girl.

At least 86% of males confess to watching animated
cartoons well into their twenties..40

For the first time in our society, women are approaching
marriage just as irresponsibly as men because their focus is
on careers and not the home. And as a result, no one is left
to tend the home..44

For this reason, you must avoid marrying a boy or girl;
instead choose a responsible man or woman.......................................45

CHAPTER 4
Humor: A man explained how he and his wife
learned to resolve their differences. He said,
"I don't try to run her life and I don't try to run mine."

When communication is the problem, wives do not
need a handy man any more than the husband needs a mother 51

A person should never be defined by
someone's image of him or her...53

When you have a longing to repair a defect
in your spouse, it is usually the mirror you're looking at.....................55

When you truly see what is wrong with yourself,
your heart is open to what is truly right..56

Your weakness becomes your greatest asset
because this is where your spouse is at his or her greater good...........57

You are of better service to your spouse with
your arms embracing rather than your fingers pointing.......................58

It is not fatal to accept criticism, but
it can prove to be lethal to accept judgment..59

You can change, if you are willing to change......................................60

Learn to confess without duress
and you'll find your marriage truly blessed...61

CHAPTER 5
Where rules exist, discipline is inevitable.

The marriage system will stand firm by itself,
but the couple will crack under the weight of their ignorance.............67

The marriage institution is completely blameless................69

Whatever is in the root is in the fruit...................70

A person should never hesitate to remove oneself from
an abusive relationship because one's life may very
well depend upon it.............................73

Don't avoid the hard and embarrassing
issues because they can save your relationship....................76

CHAPTER 6
Controlling your emotions during the pain of infidelity
is the key to avoiding the suffering of it.
Pain is inevitable but suffering is optional.

The release of anger will result
in the destruction of its root cause.........................87

If your spouse tries to project his or her weaknesses and
bad choices onto you, refuse the package and return it to sender........88

Trying to forget the past doesn't heal the pain nor
does it change the past 89

CHAPTER 7
Couples don't necessarily have financial problems;
they have discipline problems.

A good steward of money is a
responsible steward despite the amount...............96

CHAPTER 8
Good communication is a prerequisite
to experiencing a good marriage.

A major problem is that couples have a tendency to read
body language instead of listening to audible articulation................107

Body language should not be the focus of communicating;
understanding audible articulation should be the main aim
of both individuals..108

Serious problems creep into the relationship when
partners continue to misread the body language of their partners.....109

A person can say the same thing as
his or her spouse but in a different way...110

CHAPTER 9
If your priorities are out of order,
so will it be with how you spend your time.

Procrastination is the greatest thief of time.......................................117

Focused, quality time with your family is
far better than distracted, quantity time...118

Balance is the key to knowing where and
how to spend valuable time with your spouse....................................119

CHAPTER 10
Love is not a fantasy; it's a reality.

Perception, not appearance, is the key to attraction..........................129

It's not what you say, but how you say it that counts........................130

Sexual excitement is based on thought not on feelings......................131

CHAPTER 11
The secret to experiencing an exciting, healthy and
wholesome sexual relationship between
a husband and wife is to keep it a secret.

If you secretly compare, you will openly compete............................141

The lack of knowledge and information is usually what
prevents most couples from enjoying the kind of
intercourse that is mutually gratifying..142

In our culture, to be married and not experience romantic love
constitutes true deprivation..145

CHAPTER 12
Everything we do in life requires discipline.

Romantic love alone lacks the resources
to contend with conflicts successfully..156

Infatuation is as dissimilar from love as fantasy is from reality........157

The rudiments of how to love each other should be
discovered while spending valuable time together 159

Wives demonstrate love for their husbands by respecting them........160

Love your wife like you love yourself; give your life
for her and thus have no life remaining for yourself........................160

CHAPTER 13
Love should not be earned nor solicited,
but rather freely given and received.

ABOUT THE AUTHOR

Dr. Mikel Brown is an author, businessman, and religious leader who resides in El Paso, Texas, with his wife and two children. He is a Licensed Clinical Professional Counselor and Ordained Minister with over 25 years of experience. He has helped people from rocky marriages to rocketing careers. Dr. Brown's *"Just the 2 of Us Marriage Seminars"* is the most requested of all his covered subjects and they are unforgettable. He is considered a real down-to-earth speaker who has the ability to make you laugh at yourself and yet serious enough to make you change.

Dr. Brown has helped many people achieve success in marriage, business or just overcoming bad habits. He is the President and CEO of CJC Enterprises and owner and CEO of Power Communications Network, through which he conducts seminars and special events. His much sought after style of communicating and humor has made him a favorite for business conclaves and church conventions.

Beyond Ordinary

Success is Only a Thought Away

Only $11.95

ISBN: 1-930388-00-4

Beyond Ordinary
is
"The Average Person's Textbook,
The Rich Man's Manual"

If Bill Gates, Michael Jordan, Oprah Winfrey, Donald Trump, T.D. Jakes, or Mikel Brown can do it : You Can Do It, Too!

Book Review

James A. Cox, Editor-In-Chief of the Midwest Book Review says, *Beyond Ordinary - Success Is Only A Thought Away* by Mikel Brown, is a solid, 'reader friendly', self-help, self-improvement guide to overcoming setbacks and negative thinking, changing one's life and realigning one's very thoughts toward success. *Beyond Ordinary* is a strongly recommended motivational do-it-yourself manual and a page-turning guide to personal improvement and workable approach in any aspect of domestic or professional life.

For Orders:
Call: 1-915-595-1307
or *Write:* 1208 Sumac Dr. El Paso, TX 79925
www.BuildingUWealth.com

Also Available at:
www.amazon.com
www.bn.com

..Money Matters..

The Powerful Package will unleash the Financial Harvest in your lifetime!

- ➤ Start Building Your Personal Wealth Foundation
- ➤ Gain Confidence To Start Living Your Dreams
- ➤ Building Wealth Success Budget Worksheets
- ➤ Learn The Ten Commandments of Money
- ➤ Break the Mentality of "Just Enough"

Only $55.00

www.BuildingUWealth.com

Power Communications Network * 1208 Sumac Dr * El Paso, Tx 79925

Powerful Books

3 Must Have Books from Dr. Mikel Brown

God Wants You Healthy, Wealthy, & Full of Life

Your capacity to achieve, to have the life you want to have, to be the person you want to be will increase tenfold, because after reading this book you will then possess the keys to a better life. Knowing these special tips will make you more powerful and your life will change for the better.

$11.95

Developing a Champion Spirit- in just 10 Minutes for Women Only

The Greatest Gold-Mine of Easy Advice For Women Ever Crammed Into One Book

Check out the table of Contents:
- Developing the Champion in You
- Women Overcoming Self Doubt
- His Money is Your Business
- Understanding the Principle of Money
- The New Power Woman
- Secrets to Personal Success

$9.95

Developing a Champion Spirit- in just 10 Minutes for Men Only

How to Accomplish Anything You Want

Check out the table of Contents:
- Developing the Champion in You
- Changing Men in Changing Times
- The Portrait of a Leader
- Exercising Your Power to Dominate
- Principles for Commanding Mountains and Overcoming Obstacles

$9.95

www.BuildingUWealth.com
Also Available @ www.Amazon.com or www.barnesandnoble.com

www.ingramcontent.com/pod-product-compliance
Lightning Source LLC
Chambersburg PA
CBHW052029070526
44584CB00016B/1967